CW00672899

Strength In Strangers

Strength In Strangers

Lauren Britton

Published by CreateSpace

© Copyright Lauren Britton 2014

STRENGTH IN STRANGERS

All rights reserved.

The right of Lauren Britton to be identified as the author of this
work has been asserted in accordance with the Copyright, Designs
and Patents Act 1988.

No part of this publication may be reproduced, stored in a retrieval
system, or transmitted, in any form or by any means, electronic,
mechanical, photocopying, recording or otherwise, nor translated
into a machine language, without the written permission of the
publisher.

Condition of sale

This book is sold subject to the condition that it shall not, by way
of trade or otherwise, be lent, re-sold, hired out or otherwise
circulated in any form of binding or cover other than that in which
it is published and without a similar condition including this
condition being imposed on the subsequent purchaser.

ISBN 978-1-50334-938-4

Book formatted by www.bookformatting.co.uk.

Contents

To Andrew,

our family and friends,

and his donor and family

Part One

Chapter One

One week after our wedding, I was told my husband had hours to live.

"Andrew will die if you cannot get him to another hospital in the next twenty-four hours. We don't have the medical equipment to keep him alive here," said Doctor Latif.

We were on our honeymoon in the Maldives. The travel insurance company assured me they would do everything they could to get Andrew to a larger, specialist hospital in time, but Bangkok was the closest – a four-hour flight – and they could not secure a medical jet for several days. They told me there were complications with visas and landing permits.

"It is not Andrew's time," said Tholal, and I wished I could believe him, but fear and hysteria spread in my chest.

Andrew and I were married on the twenty-fifth of November on a cold bright afternoon. It was a small 1930s-themed wedding in an Art Deco cinema, the service in a registry office opposite. The guests arrived as flapper girls and gangsters, with feathers and fedoras, in paper spats and Primark pearls. They hung fake fur coats off the back of their chairs and hugged old school friends they had not seen for years.

My mum sat in the front row of white covered chairs, her grandson George beside her on his father, Iain's, lap (both dressed in matching pinstripe suits). She smiled nervously at the people she recognised, searching for seats. Across the aisle, Andrew's dad, Fraser, glowed with parental pride, and Andrew's mum, Jenny, who joked that she only cried at British sporting achievements, clutched her tissues a little too tightly. Beside her, Karen patiently listened to another of Fraser's stories. She watched her fiancé, Robert, purposefully pull the rings from his pocket and display the boxes to his brother, Andrew. They both smiled the same smile and both took a deep breath. Andrew wore a sandy-coloured tailored tweed suit and a matching cap. He nodded to his friends and straightened the handkerchief in his top pocket.

Our pageboys and flower girl walked down the aisle first, followed by my sister, and then me with my dad by my side, exhaling nervous energy, clenching his hands, smoothing his jacket, rearranging his bow tie, chattering excitedly. The photographer stumbled backwards in front of us to capture each moment with his camera.

I saw Andrew first, as we walked into the room, standing straight. The sun shone in through the tall, wide windows, and the chandelier suspended from the ceiling caught the slivers of light. The polished wooden floor echoed with our footsteps. Sixty faces turned to watch us, but Andrew's was the one I searched for first. He was composed and smiling broadly, his face illuminated with happiness.

"You look beautiful," he whispered as I stepped towards him, and he held out his hand. We turned to a surge of laughter as the smallest pageboy, who had refused to walk down the aisle with the others, toddled decisively towards us, seconds too late, stealing the show.

We listened to the registrar and repeated our vows. We promised to love each other for better, for worse, for richer, for poorer, in sickness and in health, until death do us part. He released my hand for a moment to slip his grandmother's ring onto my finger and to accept his own wedding band. We were pronounced man and wife, and we kissed and our friends cheered. This was the beginning of the rest of our lives.

We had met on the internet four years before. I had paid a £30 joining fee and picked my best photographs: me holding a coffee cup in Regent's Park with a black sparkled hat pulled down over my ears, long blonde hair, blue eyes, and freckles, muted in black and white; up close in a club with my friends pressing their faces into mine; sitting on a wall in summer, in a cheap cotton dress looking at a lake; squinting at the camera on New Year's Eve.

"I am looking for a man who will put up shelves, assemble flat-pack furniture, let me eat his dessert if it looks better than mine and laugh at my jokes. I know some nice country pubs and quirky London bars and make a mean sausage casserole." I ticked the sporty box, wants children box and likes theatre and pets boxes.

"Sporty?" said my flatmate Jane. "We've run round the park once. What quirky bars do you know? We only ever go to the Drayton, and your casserole is watery and I always have to rescue it."

"I ran a 5K with Amanda in 2005, and we once went to a Cuban bar," I said. "I can't write 'Likes eating flapjacks, watching "Step Up" dance films under a blanket on the sofa, and eating sausage soup.'"

AndrewRed1 emailed a few days later (the website had picked his pseudonym). His profile was professional and gave little away. He was twenty-eight, originally from Retford, north Nottinghamshire, but living in London. He was tall and athletic with a good straight nose and good straight teeth. He had thick, short, dark-blonde hair and blue eyes. I studied his pictures: him at a festival holding a plastic pint glass; his head in his hands in Vietnam with an oversized rucksack slung on the floor by his feet; standing by a scooter in the rain in shorts and flip-flops; diving off a boat; completing a marathon.

"You sound like you need a handyman. What sports do you enjoy? I'm intrigued by the bars," he wrote.

"Now you've done it," said Jane. "You'll come unstuck."

On an October evening we met by Ealing station. It was my first internet date. I saw him standing by the entrance as I crossed the green. He was better looking than in his pictures. We sat in the North Star pub and I drank a mulled cider. He talked about his brother, Robert, the scientist, Robert's girlfriend, Karen, his parents' new spaniel puppies, leaving his job, suffering from swine flu. I told him how many Ferrero Rochers I can eat in a minute (eight), discussed my parents' dog (who hated me), my friends and flatmates, my exaggerated sporting achievements and some carefully researched quirky bars. I sent Jane a text from the toilet. "He's nice *and* fit."

We really laughed that first night, eyes streaming, hiccupping laughter. He was kind and interesting, fun and funny. I wanted to be around him. I forgot the first date rules and texted him the minute I left.

"I had a brilliant time," or something cooler – I can't remember now.

He replied straight away, "Me too."

There was no waiting five days to respond, no playing it cool. We met again that same week and then the next and the next until the days apart became fewer and the weeks became months. He met my friends, my flatmates, my family. "We will fight and it won't always be easy, but I want to make this work," he said.

And it wasn't always easy. It wasn't always a fairy tale. He was northern and straight-talking and I was southern and sensitive. I cared what people thought and he couldn't care less. I hated confrontation and he sought it out. I was disorganised and late, while he made spreadsheets to keep to time on everyday tasks. He was highly competitive and I was used to losing. His morning run involved heart rate monitors and training plans and faster finishes. Sometimes I ran in my pyjamas. He folded his socks; I stuffed things into cupboards. He measured ingredients; I made uneducated guesses. I drove into walls, I chatted to objects, and everything I cooked was far too watery. He spent whole days cleaning his car, watched a lot of war dramas and put far too much chilli in everything he ate. He was always too hot and I was always too cold. I created an envelope of covers around my feet in our bed that he always thrashed through, kicking the cold air.

He accepted a new job with a successful hotel chain, and he was focused and ambitious and keen to climb the corporate ladder. He worked evenings and weekends and holidays and birthdays. I had worked for the same company for thirteen years and hardly progressed. I had no desire to manage two hundred people or earn a six-figure wage. I was perfectly happy, but he always wanted more for me.

"You could leave tomorrow, work for a different place."

"I don't want to leave. I'm not the same as you."

"You don't leave because you're frightened. You're so scared of everything, terrified of things going wrong, terrified of the unknown, terrified of risk."

And he was right, of course (although I'd never tell him that). What if I left my job and never found anything else? What if my new colleagues weren't as nice? What if things went wrong and I couldn't sort it out? I worried about everything, nervously twisting my hair around my fingers, rubbing my eyes and chewing my nails.

"You don't need to be scared," he'd say, swatting my hand from my face.

But I always feared the worst.

A year after we met, I left the flat I had shared with Jane and Rowland, lugging my enormous 1980s television down the steep hallway stairs, throwing my clothes, still on their hangers, into the boot of my car and carefully balancing my money plants between my knees. He brought boxes of books, his bed and his bike, and we moved to Chorleywood. He had one plate and one cup. I had a juicer and an unused cake tin. I had relied on Jane's kitchen stuff. Our friends, Kate and Mikey, helped us. It was winter and the snow was six inches thick underfoot. It was freezing cold and we hauled the book boxes and the TV up three flights of stairs. The lads struggled with dining room chairs, and Andrew's parents' old sofas, and duvets and shoes, and Kate and I stuffed things into cupboards. We ended up in the local pub and drank to our new home, our new life, our new start.

We were happy in Chorleywood. The flat was small but comfortable. We walked across the common and down by the River Chess. We ate curries in Sujoy's Indian restaurant and roast dinners in the Rose and Crown. We followed *Ultimate Pub Walk* guides into dead ends and ditches, struggling with the directions: "Take the nearly left path in a north-southerly direction by the post where a blackbird often sits." We "bed swam" in the winter to generate heat, kicking our legs and arms furiously. We walked around the Dogs Trust shelter and sponsored the saddest ones. We watched *Merlin* and *Silent Witness*, miming playing the instruments as the theme tunes played out.

We tolerated our differences, impatiently at times: Andrew snapping sharply as I dropped another glass; me saving up his comments until I erupted emotionally, taking us both by surprise.

"When you tell me I should go running, it implies you think I'm fat."

"I don't think you're fat. I'm just saying that if you were to go running you'd feel happier and more confident. You'd feel better about yourself."

"I'm not unhappy and I'm not unconfident. I feel fine about myself! Don't tell me how I feel!"

"You're being mental. I'm just saying exercise helps me when I'm feeling stressed or worried."

"I'm not being mental! I'm going to move back in with Jane. She doesn't make me go running or tell me I'm crazy!"

"You told me you liked running!"

"I do sometimes. Once a year on my own terms!"

These kinds of conversations were a regular pattern, but I never left, luckily for Jane.

We signed the register and walked along the cobbled high street to the reception venue with our guests. Rain had threatened in the morning, but never fell. The fancy dress procession behind us stumbled on the footpath, laughing and chatting excitedly. We posed for photographs in archways and under trees, on the cinema stairs and the stage and the steps.

We walked through the black cinema doors into the venue. Two sets of cinema stairs either side of the room led to the balcony. The ceiling was high above us, painted black, and an enormous chandelier hung in the middle. Black-and-white films were projected onto one empty wall. Six circular bright white tables were set for dinner with beautiful black, white and orange flowers in striking vases. An Art Deco bar, with straight black lines and polished black wood, and bottles on mirrored shelves, served cocktails in thin 1930s glasses. Art Deco paintings of bold stylised triangles and old-fashioned text covered the walls.

We greeted everyone, still hand in hand. We complimented our friends' moustaches and slicked-down hair, the drop-waisted dresses and oversized cigars. We posed for photographs on the cinema stairs and picked up glasses and put them down again, forgetting to drink. We sat at a circular table with our families. I don't remember the conversation. I tried to eat the soup while George, my nephew, spat it down his pinstriped suit. I swallowed a few pieces of chicken and ate Andrew's dessert.

Andrew's speech was well presented and professional, like a presentation at work. He thanked all the right people. The guests laughed in the right parts and cheered at the end.

Robert, in his role as best man, clicked through a PowerPoint presentation of photographs of Andrew through the years, interjected with a few family-friendly stories unlikely to offend.

"I'm only giving your speech a seven out of ten," said my friend Rach to Robert at the bar. "A best man's speech needs embarrassing drunkenness, dodgy illnesses and minor criminal activity, not falling out of a wheelbarrow aged three years old."

"A brother never tells," said Robert, "and he paid me a lot of money not to spill his secrets."

Kate was sick on champagne while Katie held her hair. Fraser's band played and he smiled broadly from the start till the end of the set. He played our first dance, Van Morrison's "Someone like you", and Andrew held me tightly and put his hat on my head. Darren and Vince led the dancing to "Gangnam Style". Robert tried to breakdance, spinning awkwardly on his side, and our friends stumbled and jumped, clutching half-drunk mojitos to "Sex on Fire". I swayed beside Karen, shouting the chorus, until Andrew grabbed me and waltzed me across the floor and held my face in his hands.

"I love you so much."

"I love you too, you drunken idiot."

Chapter Two

Two weeks before the wedding, I was sat in a shopping centre food court with my sister. It was six weeks to Christmas. I watched workmen suspend supersized baubles from the glass ceiling beams with thin metal wires.

"You know marriage is a big commitment?" she said seriously. "You know marriage is for life?"

I looked upwards and tried not to roll my eyes.

"It's just that I'm worried. We're all worried that you're not really happy. You two are so different. We're worried that you don't love him enough."

"What's enough?"

"Could you imagine a life without Andrew? If he died, could you carry on living? Is he your soulmate?"

"Ummm, yeah. I'm pretty sure I'd be OK, eventually."

"Oh God," she whispered dramatically. "If Iain died, I wouldn't be able to live. I couldn't carry on. I would be utterly and completely distraught. My entire life would be over." Her eyes began to fill with tears. "I just want that for you."

"Thanks ... I think."

Jeanette had married Iain two years before. He was a six-foot Scot with a thick Glaswegian accent. He was friendly and welcoming with a dry sense of humour. They had a six-month-old son, George – a smiley sleepless baby – and she agonised over nap times and controlled-crying plans. She was younger than me, but seemed older with her mortgage and antenatal clubs. She was generous with gifts and always chose well. She took pride in picking the perfect birthday card, and she never got it wrong. She had a sharp sense of humour and a talent for impressions of people we knew: the chap in the supermarket who analyses every item he beeps through the till, our old teachers, and people who drank in the pub. We laughed like kids at the same things: our dad's ten-year-long car project with the doors welded on upside-down, the enormous dog from down the street. We liked the same television programmes, read the same kind of books, but did not see each other often.

I *had* quietly questioned my relationship with Andrew. I had worried if I loved him enough. We were different. We disagreed. But when the music stopped at our wedding reception, and the bar was drunk dry, and we walked back along the high street to our hotel, hand in hand, I had never been happier. I wore Andrew's suit jacket across my shoulders. My feet were sore from dancing, my make-up a mess. I lost the diamond hairclip Rach had bought me (sorry when you read this), and there was red wine spilt down my dress. We laughed about Darren's dancing, discussed the speeches and the outfits. We tried to brush our teeth in the mirror, but we couldn't see straight. I forgot what I was worried about.

Andrew had proposed on a clear bright day in June, not warm enough for shorts. We were on holiday in Croyde Bay. We had stayed at a cottage B&B that had a beautiful walled garden and was owned by an elderly couple. It was a cream brick building with pale blue window frames and purple wallflowers obscuring the top-floor views. There was a thick, even lawn, spreading up to borders, filled with plants and flowers, fruit bushes and trees of different colours and heights. A mature apple tree sheltered an iron bench, the paint peeling off in strips. She made the breakfasts and he tended the garden. He fed a robin scraps of bacon from the kitchen window and she made homemade yoghurt from the fruit he picked.

We walked down a track to the village, past the seafront and along the cliff edge. We stopped for cream teas in a courtyard cafe. Andrew seemed uncharacteristically nervous, but I put it down to stress. He had been busy at work and he was training for a triathlon. We climbed over stiles and scrambled up the side of a hill until we reached the highest point. We sat on a bench and looked out to sea. We watched the surfers battling against the waves, dashing in and out of the water and dragging their boards.

He paused for a few minutes, held my hand firmly and took a deep breath.

"Wouldn't it be nice to tell our children this is where we got engaged?"

I looked at him blankly.

He stood up and knelt down.

"Will you marry me?"

"Of course," I said. It was a genuine surprise. We had not spoken about marriage.

"I was so worried," he replied. "I know I've not been so good recently. I'm sorry and I love you. I've realised what is important, and it's not work or training, it's us."

I believed him, but as our wedding day got closer, he worked harder and later. He wouldn't rest when he wasn't working. He pushed himself further physically, cycling at increasing speeds for hours each weekend, running more and more miles, swimming frenzied lengths of the local pool. He snapped when I suggested he was doing too much. I worried about our relationship. I worried that people were worried about us.

Some days before our wedding, I arrived home early from work. I knew Andrew had been back as his bag was hanging in the hall. His car was in the drive, and his work clothes were on the bed. His trainers were missing. I guessed he had walked to the gym, less than a mile from our house, and would be an hour. I made our dinner and waited for him until it went cold. When he had been gone for two hours, dark clouds descended and rain began to fall. It was cold and grim and the roads were starting to ice. The gritters ground slowly past the house. His phone went to voicemail. I called the gym to ask them to ask him if he needed a lift.

"We haven't seen him. He's not been in all week," said the receptionist, checking the register.

I waited another hour. I called his friends. I called his work, but no one had seen him. A knot of worry tightened in my stomach. He could have slipped and fallen into the canal. He could have run out in front of a car. He could have tripped and fallen and broken his foot. I got in my car and drove around the streets.

I called his mum. "I know it's probably nothing, but I don't know where he is. I'm starting to worry."

"It's completely understandable," she said calmly. "I'm sure there's an explanation, but I can see why you would worry. I'll try his phone too."

I drove to the garage, past his work, by the woods. I felt anxious and sick. Jane rang and I cried.

"I'm just so worried. He's been hours. It's so unlike him. I just don't know what to do. I need to check his running routes."

"Stay there, I'll come over. Don't walk the streets on your own." She hung up sharply and I tried to think straight. I drove back to our street.

As I locked the car door, Andrew appeared at the end of the street. He was soaked through, wearing running trainers, a T-shirt, shorts and a sodden backpack. It was freezing cold and his face was flushed. I threw myself at him in rage and relief.

"Where the hell have you been?"

"Hey," he said, stepping back to see my tearful face, "why so emotional? I've just run to the big gym and swum a few lengths."

"The big gym is ten miles away! You've been gone for four hours. You never left a note, your phone was turned off, and I've worried myself sick."

"My battery ran out. I didn't realise the time. I'm sorry," he said.

He held me by the shoulders.

"Nothing is going to happen to me. You need to stop worrying. You cannot spend your whole life thinking something bad is going to happen."

Chapter Three

We set off for our honeymoon two days after our wedding. We still had hangover shadows blurring our brains. We were tired but excited; it was the holiday of our dreams. Andrew had booked a beachfront villa on a beautiful island in the Maldives, owned by the company he worked for. The brochure showed bright white sand and clear blue sea. It would be two weeks of relaxing, with no worries or distractions. Andrew left his work laptop in our lounge and promised not to check his emails.

I tried not to twist my hair and not to worry about the flight. We parked my car in the long-stay car park and tried to commit to memory where we had left it for when we returned in two weeks' time.

The plane was half full. After eating, I moved to stretch out across the four empty seats in front of our own. I was dozing uncomfortably, the seatbelts digging into my side, when Andrew nudged me, leaning over the top of the seat behind.

"I've been sick," he said sadly. "I feel really bad."

"You had a wine and a beer," I replied. "It's probably that. Do you want me to get you a cool towel or a toothbrush?"

"It's OK," he said, shifting back into his seat. "I'll just sit here quietly and see if the nausea passes."

He didn't nudge me again. Every so often I would peer through the gap in the chairs to check he was sleeping. His breathing was even. For once, I wasn't worried.

We arrived on the main island, Malé, around ten hours later. The airport was busy with tourists and travel reps. We found the speedboat station for our island resort. Andrew was tired and still felt sick but he put on a brave face. We boarded the boat and he tried to help carry my bag, despite struggling to carry his own. We looked out across the sea and saw the islands in the distance. It was warm but slightly overcast. A light breeze whipped through my hair and salt spray struck our faces as the speedboat slashed sharply through the waves. I worried about the five-day forecast. I worried Andrew wasn't wearing enough sun cream. I worried the journey would make his nausea worse, but he smiled and held my hand. It took an hour from the mainland to the island resort.

Tholal took my hand and steadied my footing. I didn't know his name then. He was one of five resort employees in white T-shirts and cream shorts helping tourists off the boat. He had a wide Maldivian smile and bright brown eyes. He was taller than his colleagues, with broad shoulders and short black hair. He drove us to our chalet in a beach buggy.

"It is one mile around the island," he said, proudly pointing to the shore.

The wheels left defined tracks in the fine white sand, and the palm trees, like lamp posts, were spread evenly along the paths. The sun burned through the clouds and the sky was clear blue. Only eighty other couples resided at the resort. They sat on the seafront seats and beside the pristine pools. Waiters in white shirts carried cocktails on trays, and one lone surfer pulled his board from the sea. People with snorkels searched for colourful fish, and tanned newlyweds lounged on deckchairs, their fingers entwined.

Our chalet was situated in a row of ten, opening out on to the beach. It was painted white with a large white bed and white marble floors, simple but luxurious. A huge widescreen television faced the bed. There was a juicer with fresh fruit balanced beside it, a bottle of champagne and two flutes on the side. Thick fluffy towels were folded on the bed and beautiful flowers scented the room. The bathroom was white marble with a large sunken bath and an outdoor shower bathed in sun. Patio doors opened out onto decking, where a hammock hung from two trees and a cushioned sofa was situated in the shade. The sea was a few steps across the sand, and water chalets on stilts rose up out of the water. It was a peaceful paradise.

"I feel much better now," Andrew said firmly, falling back onto the bed. "I just need a little nap."

I walked the seconds to the sea and left my flip-flops on the shore. I took some pictures on my phone. When I got back to the room, Andrew was vomiting in the outdoor shower. I soaked a flannel in cold water, squeezed toothpaste on his toothbrush and passed them to him. The shower gels and shampoos were in small coloured terracotta jars balanced on the ledge. I inspected the contents and rubbed the moisturiser into my hands.

"That's better," he said, and then stumbled to the bed. I put the bin from the bathroom beside his head and squashed all the fruit into a sweet pithy juice.

"Vitamins."

"I'm OK," he said, "just still slightly hung-over. I can't stomach anything but water. I just need to sleep."

I sat on the decking and felt a little frustrated that our holiday had not started well. I uploaded the view to Facebook on my phone. "First day of honeymoon and Andrew being sick."

"Sad face," replied my friends, and, "in sickness and in health."

He was sick every few hours and all through the night. I ordered him a clear chicken soup but he brought it back up. He sipped on some water but he couldn't keep it down.

"Please stop worrying," he said. "It's just a twenty-four-hour bug. Please leave me to sleep. I don't need you hovering over me."

I wasn't worried. He had been sick like this before, and it always passed by the morning. I sat in the sun and flicked through my books.

When he woke, his skin was grey and dark circles engulfed his eyes. He was thirsty but couldn't drink. I swapped the bin by the bed full of vomit, and swilled it out in the shower.

"Should we call the doctor?" I said.

He could hardly speak now; his voice was hoarse, and he could hardly lift his head from the pillow.

"I'll be OK," he said. "I just need to hold down some food."

So I waited. I wish I hadn't waited. I ordered plain rice, and he ate a spoonful and sipped a cool glass of coke. I felt hopeful he was recovering. He walked towards the doors and drew a breath of fresh air. We watched Vin Diesel films and he slipped into sleep. I read my book in the room and planned the things we would do on the island once he was better. I soaked flannels in the sink and put them in the fridge to cool. I laid them beside the unopened bottle of champagne and retrieved them to place across his forehead.

In the morning his eyes were sunken. He had been sick all night. His lips were cracked and his body was weak. I called for the resort doctor and he came straight away.

I never knew his name. Everyone called him "The Doctor", even his friends. He was in his twenties, smartly dressed in a white shirt and cream chinos. His skin was light and his eyes were black and sincere.

"Your English is good," I said.

"I was born in Derby," he said, smiling, pulling a thermometer from his bag.

"Another northerner," said Andrew. "I feel strangely reassured."

He attached Andrew to a drip. Andrew was so dehydrated that he struggled to insert the canular into a vein. It lasted for four hours, and I watched the drip intently: the gradual drip, drip of the fluid along the tube.

"If it stops, it's not good," said The Doctor. "Give me a call. I'll return in a few hours and see how he gets on."

True to his word, he returned in three hours and changed the drip.

"If you don't feel better after the next drip, we need to think about taking you to the hospital on the mainland."

I feared the hospital would be crowded and dirty and full of infection.

I shook my head. "I'm sure he'll be fine."

"I will," Andrew agreed, "once I get some fluids."

The Doctor came six times to change the drip. Andrew slept with his arm resting on the side of the bed. He pushed his drip like a Zimmer frame to the outdoor shower and vomited furiously time after time.

His fingers became so thin, his wedding ring slid off.

"I'm scared I'll lose it," he said.

I put it on the bedside table.

I rang his mum from outside. "I think it's probably the norovirus," she said calmly. "Several of my friends have had it, and it can last forty-eight hours. Try not to worry. It's just such a shame."

At nine o'clock that night, he told me he was struggling to breathe. We were lying on the bed in pyjamas; we hadn't dressed for days.

"I think I need some oxygen. I can't breathe."

I rang The Doctor. "Pack a bag for him," he said.

I pulled on a black jersey maxi dress, a black cardigan and flip-flops and stuffed his shorts and a T-shirt into a plastic bag. I didn't brush my hair or take my handbag. I grabbed my phone and my wallet. I forgot the key to the room. I left his ring on the side table.

"Take the passports from the safe and a little bit of cash," Andrew said, as he hauled himself from the bed and shuffled towards the door, still pushing the drip.

The beach buggy we had arrived in was parked across from the porch. The Doctor stepped down; Tholal was driving. He smiled warmly and helped Andrew into his seat, balancing the drip beside him.

"I think it's time to take him to the hospital," The Doctor said calmly. "We'll be a few hours, and Andrew might have to stay overnight. Do you really want to come?"

"Of course," I said. "I won't leave him."

Chapter Four

A small boat to the mainland was waiting at the pier. The bar and restaurant behind us glowed in the darkness, and the warm sound of laughter and glasses carried across the sand. Ahead it was almost pitch black; there were only a few lights in the distance reflected in the sea. I stepped aboard, and Tholal and The Doctor assisted Andrew. The engine started: a loud and constant drone; I had to shout to be heard. We accelerated into the darkness and I had no idea if the speedboat driver knew where he was. I couldn't see anything further than what was in front of my face. Waves crashed across the side of the boat and lapped at our feet. The boat rocked and I was thrown across the plastic seats. I scanned the inside for life jackets and clung to the side. Tholal was sat next to Andrew; he steadied his drip and held him straight. No one spoke.

We collided with another enormous wave and Andrew turned to vomit off the edge of the boat. Instinctively I reached for him but he pushed me away. Tholal unscrewed a bottle of water and gently passed it to him. He smiled at me warmly.

"How long?" I shouted, the wind biting my face, the sea soaking my skirt.

"About an hour," yelled The Doctor.

The engine sound changed as the driver hurtled faster ahead. The darkness engulfed us. I was terrified we would crash. I took deep breaths and twisted my hair. I needed the toilet.

It took fifty minutes.

An ambulance was waiting at the dock. Tholal and The Doctor helped Andrew off the boat. The paramedics eased him onto a stretcher.

"I'm OK," he said, "I don't need a stretcher." But they didn't understand. They strapped him to the bed, clipping the belts across his waist.

I sat in the front of the ambulance and looked out of the windscreen. I recognised parts of the mainland. The island was 5km² in size, but 100,000 people inhabited the small space. The streets were crowded, adults and children, women in headscarves and long skirts, men in suits and light cream trousers. Neon lights flashed above electrical shopfronts, and I saw stalls selling coconuts. Motorbikes lined the sides of the streets, parked in every possible place, packed closely together, handlebars overlapping. Tall pastel-coloured buildings in pinks and yellows and blues stretched to the sky, their windows wide. You could see the sea from the end of almost every road. Cars and many motorcycles forced past the ambulance without pausing. They pulled from junctions and raced across the roads. No one stopped to let us through. The air was thick with shouts and horns, food smells and exhaust fumes. It was busy and buzzy. Andrew's stretcher slid across the back as we screeched around corners and I understood why they had strapped him in. I still needed the toilet.

The hospital was a large white stone building facing the sea, surrounded by red railings with hundreds of motorbikes resting against the surrounding wall. The ambulance pulled swiftly into the grounds and the paramedics transferred Andrew to a wheelchair and then pushed him through to the accident and emergency reception area. It was blindingly bright inside. The thick strip lighting hummed. There were green signs in Maldivian script stuck to the white walls. A lady sat behind a high desk, a headscarf pulled around her face. She considered her computer and directed people through the doors surrounding the room. People queued and jostled to the front. Elderly men slumped in metal chairs against the wall, and children climbed across and under benches beside the chairs or clung to their parents and cried noisily. It was busy and loud. I was tired and hot. There was no air conditioning. No one spoke English.

The Doctor spoke to the receptionist, and she pointed to a clear glass door. Andrew was pushed through to the emergency room.

There were rows of hospital beds side by side; thin green polyester curtains separated each one.

On the left side there was space for one red plastic chair, tightly wedged in. Andrew was directed to a bed and I squeezed into the chair. The Doctor spoke to the nurses stationed at the far end of the room. There were peeling posters showing fresh fruit and smoking warnings on the white walls. Tholal hovered beside The Doctor. He was still smiling.

On the left side of Andrew, an elderly lady cried quietly in pain. Her face was creased, her hair grey, and her husband consoled her in a language I couldn't understand. On the other side, two teenage girls in headscarves and jeans whispered happily; neither one looked unwell. Patients watched us warily, surprised to see us in the state hospital. There were no other tourists.

The resort doctor returned to the bed. "They want to do a few tests."

"Do you know where the toilet is?" I asked hopefully, crossing my legs.

"Tholal will show you," he said. "He knows the hospital well."

Tholal smiled his wide smile. "Come this way," he said.

He pointed to a scratched white door, the paint flaking in strips. Liquid on the floor lapped over my flip-flops, soaking the hem of my dress. The sink was stained almost black, thick with lime scale; the taps were rusted and brown. The toilet was low to the ground. There was a shower head attached to a hose beside the bowl, no toilet paper. I can keep holding, I thought. We won't be here long.

I returned to Andrew. He was sat on the side of the bed, his feet touching the floor.

"I feel fine now," he said, smiling, "but they have to do some tests."

I rang his mum and explained the situation. She was calm and reassuring.

"Just keep us updated," she said. "You're both doing really well."

The hospital's junior doctors arrived at Andrew's bed. Three confident young men, they wore smart jeans and trainers and button-down check shirts. They spoke little English and translated through the resort doctor what they intended to do. They lifted Andrew's shirt and stuck heart monitor stickers across his chest. They inspected the canular and measured his temperature. It all seemed very normal. They kept the curtains open. Nurses in navy headscarves moved carefully across the room, collecting blood samples, carrying injections and forms. It was quiet and calm. The clock on the wall showed nearly midnight. It was dark outside but the fluorescent strip lighting burned my tired eyes.

The lead hospital doctor, Doctor Latif, joined the group. He had a thick dark beard obscuring half his face and small half-frame glasses perched on the end of his nose. He wore chinos and a light shirt, his sleeves rolled up. The other doctors looked to him with admiration and respect, waiting for his reaction every time they spoke. His phone kept ringing and he pulled it from his pocket to answer every call. He oversaw everything in the emergency room. He was older than the others, with comprehensible English. He shook the hand of the doctor from the resort. They spoke for some seconds, and then Doctor Latif and the junior doctors moved on to the next bed. Andrew stretched out on top of the sheets and closed his eyes.

"They want to keep him in until the morning. They want to check for swine flu," said the resort doctor. "I need to return to the island but Tholal will stay with Andrew and bring him back in the morning by boat. You can stay here or come back with me, but I will warn you, you won't get any sleep here."

"I'll stay with Andrew," I said. "I don't want to leave him. I don't care if I don't sleep. We'll sleep on the beach in the morning when we get back to the resort."

"Fine," said The Doctor. "I'll see you in the morning then. Tholal will look after you."

I looked across at Tholal and he smiled and agreed. He pulled up a chair and sat next to me. He was tall, maybe six foot, with an open easiness that made me feel calm. He relaxed into the chair, slumping back, stretching his legs.

"I'm Lauren, this is Andrew."

"I'm Tholal, nice to meet you," he replied. His English was good but he still searched for some words before he spoke.

He told us he was twenty-seven. He laughed when I said we were thirty-two.

"You look so young," he said.

I smiled and nudged Andrew. "I told you I look youthful. It's all those vitamins."

Tholal liked football and he followed English teams. He lived in Malé and commuted to the island resort every day. He had worked for the hotel company for six months and before that he had been in the army. He had visited many of his friends from his unit in the hospital so he knew it well. He had never been to England, but he had been to China on exercises. He loved his motorbike and rode everywhere.

"The Doctor said we won't get much sleep. I'm sorry you have to stay with us," I said.

"In the army, sometimes I didn't sleep for three days. It's fine."

"Thank you," I said.

"Are you thirsty?" he asked, standing up and scraping his chair along the floor.

I nodded. "Thank you."

He left to get some water and I rested my head on the side of Andrew's bed and closed my eyes.

Suddenly, alarms were ringing, and they echoed through the ward. The monitors above Andrew flashed red and fast. I jumped to my feet. He looked OK. Every doctor rushed to his bed. A nurse urgently ushered me out of the way and sharply swiped the curtains shut. I couldn't see what was happening; someone shouted a few words, and Doctor Latif ran across the ward. I tried to push through the curtain but a nurse held her arm out to stop me.

"What's happening?" I asked, trying to keep my voice calm.

She looked at me blankly; she couldn't understand. She picked up a chair and motioned for me to sit down a foot from the curtain.

Tholal returned, holding two bottles of water.

"One for Andrew and one for you," he said smiling, pulling up a chair beside me.

"Something is happening," I said. "I don't know what's going on. No one understands me. Please can you ask what's going on?"

"Of course," he said, and he approached a nurse.

I watched his face tighten and his smile start to fade. He repeated a few words and the nurse nodded. I tried to push through the curtains again, but again they held me back. Andrew's feet hung off the bed. They looked grey and lifeless.

"We must go to the office now," urged Tholal, grabbing my arm.

"Why, what office? What do you mean?" I asked.

"We need to pay money for the doctors to treat him," he replied, carefully choosing his words.

"Why? What's wrong? What's happened?" I heard panic in my voice.

Doctor Latif stepped towards me and he clasped his hands together tightly. He stooped a little to look me in the eye.

"Your husband has had a heart attack," he said simply. "We will do all we can."

I looked at Tholal and then back at the doctor.

"I don't understand," I whispered.

"Your husband has had a heart attack," he repeated. "We have given him drugs to stabilise his condition, but I need your permission to do a cardioversion if the drugs stop working."

I couldn't think straight. The room had started to spin. I saw the curtains and nurses move out of focus. The bright lights were blinding, and the bile rose in my throat. The heat, the airlessness, I struggled to stand. I grasped my phone tightly in my hand. Heart attack. The word wouldn't register. It didn't make sense. He wasn't old or unhealthy. He didn't smoke or drink to excess.

"I need your permission to defibrillate him," Doctor Latif said. "We may need to shock him to stabilise his heart."

"I don't know," I whispered. "I don't know. I don't know."

"There are risks," he said patiently. His phone had begun to ring.

I looked to Tholal, and he held my hand.

"I need to ask his parents," I said, shaking. "I don't know. I don't know."

Jenny answered the phone on the first ring. I tried to explain, but I couldn't form the words. I passed the phone to the doctor.

"Please tell them," I whispered. "I can't tell them. I don't understand."

"Your son has arrhythmia," said Doctor Latif. "We use this term to describe an abnormal heart rhythm. His heart rate rose to 190 beats per minute and then stopped because it was working too hard. We stabilised him with drugs. If it happens again, we will need to defibrillate him. I need an assurance that this is OK."

He passed the phone back to me.

"Lauren," said Jenny, "you have to trust the doctors. They must do the procedure if it will save his life. Please let us know what happens. We will start looking at flights to come to you. Please try and stay calm as best you can. You are doing so well. Fraser and I are here for you. Please keep calm. Please trust the doctors."

Doctor Latif spoke urgently to Tholal.

"Do what you need to do," I said. "Please don't let him die."

"We must go the office," said Tholal, still holding my hand. "They cannot treat him until you pay. I will take you there."

I turned to face him. He still held Andrew's bottle of water, and he put his hands on my shoulders.

"Lauren, we need to do this now."

I pulled myself from his grip and stumbled towards the toilet. I stared at my face in the mirror for a second. I was pale, my eyes sunken, hair matted across my face. I couldn't cry. I couldn't think. Nothing felt real. I sat on the toilet and tried to steady myself. I vomited on the floor in front of me and then frantically searched for paper to clear the mess. There was only the shower and I sprayed it across the floor. I wanted it clean; I couldn't leave it dirty.

Outside, I heard Tholal insistently rapping on the door.

"Lauren, we must hurry. Please hurry," he begged.

I staggered from the toilet and he took my arm.

"The toilet, it's a mess," I murmured as he guided me from the ward. We walked through the empty hospital. Our footsteps echoed across the floor. It was eerily quiet, a maze of corridors and stairs, white stone floors and white walls, buzzing strip lighting, hot and airless. He half-walked, half-dragged me, neither of us speaking, towards the office.

He spoke urgently to the woman sitting behind the desk. She tapped something into the computer and then looked at me warily.

"You need to fill in Andrew's details: date of birth, address, full name," Tholal translated.

My hand was shaking as I took the pen. She scanned the form and spoke to Tholal again.

"You must pay five thousand," he said.

"I looked at her and she nodded. "Five thousand," she said with a strong accent.

"The doctors cannot treat him unless you pay," Tholal reiterated.

We had travel insurance that I thought we would never use, free with our bank account. I had never read the small print. I vaguely checked it before we left. I pulled my bank card from my bag and shakily dialled the number into my phone. The battery was depleting. I ignored the two bars. It was 4am in the UK and it rang and rang. Eventually I spoke to someone who said they would put me through.

Tholal had started to transfer his weight from foot to foot. He clenched his hands and reassured the receptionist. He anxiously listened to my phone call, trying to make out my words.

"You have the money?" he asked. "Please hurry."

The tallest junior doctor arrived and hovered around Tholal. He drew him away from me. Tholal looked back at me nervously. I saw him raise his hands to the doctor as if to say "wait".

"I need to take some security questions," said the insurance company's customer services employee. "It may take a few minutes."

"My husband has had a heart attack. I'm in a hospital in the Maldives. I don't think they'll treat him until I get the money sorted."

"OK," she said calmly. "I will do everything I can. Please don't panic. I am here to help."

I answered the questions quickly, but I needed to ask Tholal for advice. He ran to get the hospital phone number and the names of the doctors involved. He spelt out the location, the postcode and the names.

"We need to confirm with the hospital," she said, "and then we can assess your case. I can't tell you right now if we can pay, but I will keep you informed every step of the way."

I hung up and faced Tholal.

"They will pay now?" he asked.

"Not yet, they need to check," I replied.

His face was full of fear. He relayed this to the junior doctor and the doctor shook his head. Tholal pleaded. He tried to explain. I couldn't understand but it was perfectly clear. Tholal paused for a moment and then spoke to the receptionist again. Eventually, she nodded and walked away from her desk. She returned with a piece of paper. He grabbed a pen and signed the form. He shouted to the doctor and he nodded and raced towards the ward.

"It's all OK," he said, taking my hand, leading me back through the corridors. "The money is sorted, so they can help Andrew now."

"How? Thank you. What did you say?"

"I am a resident of Malé. I signed my house over as an assurance you will get them the money by the morning," he said.

"You will get them the money by the morning?"

"Of course," I said, not really registering at the time what he had done. "Thank you. Of course I will get the money. Thank you."

"We must speak to the lead doctor now," he said, leading me back.

Chapter Five

The curtains were still drawn around Andrew's bed. A junior doctor emerged from behind them. He spoke to Tholal for a second.

"He wants you," he said.

The doctors pulled the curtains back. Andrew was sat bolt upright in the bed. His face was grey and his eyes were wild. He had drips in each arm. His bright yellow T-shirt was ripped down the middle, the two halves hanging loosely by his side. Heart monitor stickers were stuck all over his chest.

"What the fuck's going on?" he shouted. "Lauren, what's going on? We were talking and then I heard the alarms and then no one is saying anything. I can't understand anyone. No one speaks English! When can we go home?"

"It's alright," I said, reaching for his hand. I didn't know what to say. I didn't want to scare him. He had no idea. "They just need to do a few tests, I think," I said, steadying my voice, steadying myself.

"I need the toilet," he shouted. "They want to put a catheter in. I don't want a catheter. What the hell's going on?"

It was hard to believe that he'd had a heart attack, he spoke so coherently. Maybe they had made a mistake? Maybe I didn't understand? The monitors started to flash again, and the doctors ran to the bed. I watched them push infusions into his arm, silence the alarms, call for help. His eyes rolled back into his head and he fell back onto the bed.

I looked, terrified, at the doctor, my heart racing with sheer panic.

"He is stable but sedated," said Doctor Latif. "We must keep him calm and move him to the intensive care unit."

"I'm here. It's OK," I said, gripping Andrew's lifeless hand.

The doctors and porters pushed his bed through the double doors of the emergency room and into the large metal lifts. I wanted to stay beside him but there was no space. We were directed to the stairs. Tholal and I took the steps two at a time. The intensive care corridor was dark at the top with only one small window at the end. Cold metal benches lined the sides, single seats separated by armrests so you couldn't stretch across them. Large white fans were suspended high on the wall, whirring irritably, generating a vague breeze. The air was heavy and hot.

Worried relatives tried to rest on the uncomfortable seats, bags at their feet, phones in their hands, not making eye contact. People unplugged the fans to use the sockets to charge their phones. The handsets hung like pendulums. The pale blue painted ward doors stayed firmly shut. Christmas decorations hung above the circumcision ward.

"They are for the boys," said Tholal, pointing to the streamers. I didn't ask anymore.

I texted a few friends and family with the little battery I had left. I could hardly press the keys, my hands were shaking so violently. I sent a few alarming and distressing jumbled-up words.

We sat by the door marked ICU (intensive care unit) and waited. We hardly spoke. My teeth chattered like it was freezing, but it was stiflingly hot. Tholal passed me the water for Andrew and encouraged me to sip. I hunched over, twisted my hair, but couldn't form any thoughts. A Tannoy chimed like a supermarket announcement, and a woman said a few words in Maldivian. The relatives around us looked up while they listened.

"It's us," said Tholal standing. "They said Andrew's name and bed number."

He led me through a pale blue door, confidently pushing it open. We walked into a small room painted bright yellow. There were health advice posters in English peeling off every wall and a grey padded treatment couch across the far end. A locked door to the left led onto the small intensive care ward. There was a yellow line painted across the floor a foot from the door and dusty pairs of shoes abandoned behind it. In front of the line there were pairs of blue hospital flip-flops.

"You have to change your shoes for infection," said Tholal, slotting his feet into an empty pair. He walked towards the locked door and rapped sharply on the window. A nurse in a navy headscarf peered at us. She disappeared into the background and Doctor Latif opened the door. He looked at me carefully, considering his words.

"The medicine is not working. We will need to do the cardioversion. You understand?"

"Cardioversion?"

"Defibrillate him. Shock him."

"If it doesn't work, is he going to die?"

The doctor moved his head from side to side. "There are risks. We will call for you on the Tannoy when the procedure is complete."

I took a sharp breath and Tholal held me upright and helped me back to the corridor. I couldn't walk for myself. My legs wouldn't work. We sat side by side. We didn't speak. I was shaking violently: my teeth chattered, and my hands shook. I felt light-headed and nauseous. Tholal reached to steady my hand. I wondered if he was praying as he closed his eyes and whispered words to himself. I began to cry.

"Please don't cry," he said, turning in his seat to face me. "It is not time to cry."

"I can't do this. I can't do this. I'm not strong enough."

"You can," he said. "You are strong. You are so strong. You can do this. I will look after you."

The minutes that passed were the longest of my life. I prayed. I wished. I bargained for Andrew's life. "I will do anything," I whispered, "just keep him safe, don't let him die."

So many thoughts went through my mind as I waited. I imagined Doctor Latif telling me they had done all they could do. I imagined losing him. I imagined hearing he was dead. I could hardly breathe; my words came out in sobs.

I called my sister, shakily, my fingers sliding over the keys of my phone.

"I said to you I wasn't sure if I loved him enough," I cried. "I said if he died I would be OK. I won't be OK. I won't be OK. I shouldn't have said those things. My bluff has been called. He can't die. He can't die. I do love him. I love him more than anything. I love him so much. I love him enough."

I heard her draw a breath; her voice began to break.

"You didn't mean those things. Don't think those things. Don't ever think that again. I know you love him. He knows you love him. Just try and keep calm. I'll keep talking to you until you know what's happened, Mum and Dad are coming round here. We love you so much."

"I love you all too, but I've got no battery." The line cut dead. I listened to the emptiness. The phone pressed against my ear. My only link to home was lost.

"My phone," I said. "The battery has run out. I don't know what to do. What can I do?"

Tholal spoke to the people waiting. A young man sitting at the other end of the corridor delved into his bag and passed Tholal his charger. I hung my phone above me and plugged it into the fan socket. What would I have done without Tholal?

"How long will you stay?" I asked.

"I won't leave you," he said.

Every time the Tannoy sounded I looked at his face and tried to read his expression. Were they asking for us? He shook his head the first time, the second, the third.

On the fourth Tannoy call, he leapt to his feet and raced to the door. I trailed, terrified, behind.

A nurse was waiting by the door. She spoke to Tholal in an urgent tone. His face was serious. He gritted his teeth. His facial muscles tensed.

"Please, tell me," I whispered. I grabbed his arm.

"Stable," exhaled Tholal. "He is stable. It worked."

"Can I see him?" I said, and the nurse nodded and led me through to the intensive care ward.

It was a small white room with beds divided by green curtains in a circle around a central desk. Nurses in navy blue headscarves and floor-length skirts walked purposefully around the room, stopping at the desk to pick up paperwork. They wore surgical gloves. They smiled warmly at me. One of them gently took my arm.

Andrew was sleeping peacefully. He was wearing a hospital gown. He had drips in his wrists and there were bottles and sachets hung above his head. He had heart monitors on his chest and a clip on his finger. I looked at the monitor to the side of his bed. I watched his heart rate stabilise and maintain an even speed.

Tholal stood by the desk. He spoke to the nurses at length. A nurse gave him some invoices and a printed list on a small slip of paper in English: medicines, saline pouches, three bottles of water, one toothbrush, one toothpaste, bed sheets, one pillow, one pillowcase, one plate, one spoon, one set of pyjamas, three liquid meal packs.

"We cannot stay much longer," he said. "It is not the visiting times. We cannot see him again until 11am. We must buy these things now. We must pay for his medicines. I have given them my mobile number and they will call if it is important."

I looked at the list. "Do they not provide this stuff?"

"Of course not," he said.

I took the NHS for granted. "And what if you can't pay?"

He shrugged his shoulders. We walked down the stairs and into the foyer. He took me to the pharmacy and the hospital shop. He negotiated for the goods and I paid with the few notes I had taken from the safe. It felt like a dream. I waited to wake up. We returned to the corridor and passed the bags to the nurses.

The insurance company called.

"We can cover the costs of the treatment," said the lady on the end of the phone. "We'll investigate moving Andrew to another specialist hospital, but we will speak to the doctors first over the next few hours. We'll be in touch."

"They've paid," I said to Tholal. "Thank you again."

"It was nothing. No problem," he said. "It's late. You must try to sleep."

"I can't sleep."

"Please try," he said, "if only for an hour."

"What about you?"

"I told you before. I was in the army. Sometimes I didn't sleep for days. I will stay awake and listen for the Tannoy."

"You won't leave me."

"I told you I will not leave you," he said.

I kicked my flip-flops off and curled awkwardly into the chair. I felt the cold metal armrests against my cheek. I shut my eyes. I was wide awake. I sat back up and shuffled up and down the hall. I stood by the window at the end of the corridor and pressed my face against the glass. Tholal watched me carefully, like a sentry. He handed me water and offered me sugary snacks.

"Have you ever experienced anything like this before?"

"No, not like this. I can't stay still."

"I know."

"I feel like I need to do something to help him."

"Keep yourself strong, eat, drink and rest. That is how you will help him."

Chapter Six

Robert, Andrew's brother, rang me around 3am. I don't know what time it was at home.

"I have been in touch with the British consulate and the insurance company too. We will get through this. Anything you need, Karen and I are here. I know we're a long way away but we'll do everything we can."

I had met Robert and Karen some four years before. Andrew and I had travelled to Leicester, where they both worked in cancer research for the university. Rob was older than Andrew, shorter and darker haired. He was relaxed and laughed easily. He liked his food and talked a lot about sandwiches. He ran and swam as much as Andrew. He wore orange trainers and patterned shirts and cooked a chilli with thirty-three spices. He made ice cream with liquid nitrogen borrowed from the lab and played for a county hockey team that was often in trouble for complaining about the teas.

Karen had three nieces and she saw them as often as she could. Her family were important to her. She sat in the same seats every Saturday with her dad and her brother at Highbury, her striped scarf wound tightly around her neck. She had light red hair and a thick long fringe. She had bright blue eyes and a warm welcoming smile. She was successful and hardworking. She had recently become a professor in her field of cell research. She worked late at her laptop to finish her papers and was careful and calm.

On our first meeting, we watched the brothers play squash from the glass-fronted cafe of a Leicester leisure centre. It was Andrew's ambition to beat Robert but he was never quite quick enough. They played the same sports and were highly competitive, but Robert always won. I remember Fraser telling me that he offered both boys the opportunity to play the guitar, but Robert chose not to as he wanted Andrew to have something that was all his own. I told Robert and he laughed. "I don't remember that. I would probably have been better though."

There was an easy understanding between them. They spoke often and honestly and were supportive and encouraging of each other's achievements. They were close friends, and Robert understood Andrew better than anyone else.

"Are they quite alike?" I asked Karen, as they skidded across the court chasing the small ball.

"Yes and no," she said. "I think Rob is more like their mum: measured, scientific, calm, less emotional. Andrew is more like Fraser: creative, compassionate, a little more emotional. You haven't met their parents yet, have you? You'll like them a lot."

I met his parents the following day. They lived in the market town of Retford. His mum, Jenny, had made quiche and tea in the pot. They both clung on to their spaniels' collars to stop them from jumping. Jenny was an attractive older lady with short blonde grey hair in the style of Helen Mirren. She was sensibly dressed in dog-walking clothes, thick woollen socks and hardwearing jeans. She had the same blue eyes as Andrew and a strong Newcastle accent.

Fraser was from Stoke Poges. He was smartly dressed with thick hair. He had glasses and a chuckly laugh. They were both retired teachers. Jenny walked their dogs with her friends – "the ladies from Lound" – and volunteered at the local nature reserve. She briskly led seventy-year-old "silver strollers" through the marshland, unused to her pace, and crossed off the birds in her birdwatching book. She was a good squash player but her knees hurt now, and she cooked delicious dinners from scratch. She read extensively and we talked about books. She was very like Andrew, strong-willed and opinionated but thoughtful and kind.

Fraser played golf; he played guitar and sang in his popular local blues band. He researched every item he bought on the internet and advised local people at the Citizens Advice Bureau. He rarely walked the dogs. He got stressed when they ran away (which they often did) and he watched a lot of Sky Sports. A teacher of sociology, he was confident and theatrical. He was proud of his sons, and their certificates of achievements and photographs were stuck to the kitchen wall. He was supportive and positive about everything they did. When Andrew felt down, he always rang his dad, and Fraser listened and advised without judging. When Andrew was younger, he struggled with certain subjects at school and Fraser had written him encouraging notes. Andrew never forgot this. Fraser told him he loved him at the end of every call and hugged him tightly every time he left.

"It's like he's never going to see me again," said Andrew.

Chapter Seven

Tholal and I sat in the corridor until the Tannoy sounded. Each time it did I had to buy medicines, or pay for procedures or food. My money ran out. I handed over my credit card. I had no idea of the exchange rate. I didn't care. We carried the boxes back to the yellow room and watched through the window as they administered the drugs.

The sun rose through the window at the end of the hall. It was 7am and I was sweaty and dishevelled.

"Are you hungry?" he asked. I shook my head.

"You need to eat," he said.

"I can't leave here. What if he wakes up and wants me? What if they call? What if he gets worse or they need something?"

"They have my mobile number," he replied, rising from his seat. "They will call me if they need us. Let's go to the canteen."

I followed him along the corridor, down the stone steps, across the huge empty waiting room with blank display screens and rows and rows of seats, past the shop and the pharmacy, down a sloped stone path with green railings and out to the canteen.

The canteen was a gravelled area at the back of the hospital. To the right of the path was a glass-sided building, like a greenhouse, filled with red plastic chairs and unstable white tables. Doctors, nurses, relatives and cleaners picked up pre-plated food displayed behind a glass cabinet: curries, curried pastries, spiced bread, dried sausages and hard boiled eggs. A small fridge of cold drinks hummed in the heat.

Outside, the sun throbbed through the leafless trees. There was no shade. In the middle, a tall mound of yellow and green coconuts, built like a bonfire, threatened to spill out across the gravel if one dislodged. Behind, there was a low white stone wall facing the clear blue sea, which was scattered with boats. It was a bright and beautiful early morning. People and motorbikes filled the streets.

Tholal found an empty table and beckoned me to sit down. He brought a sausage, a boiled egg, a thin piece of white bread and a strong cup of coffee.

"I won't have anything," I said. I couldn't swallow. My throat wouldn't work.

"You must eat."

"I have no money left."

"I will buy it for you."

He picked a coconut from halfway down the tower. I waited for them to fall like Jenga bricks, but the stack stayed steady. A waiter drilled a hole in the top and pierced a straw through the flesh. Tholal proudly presented it to me.

"You will like this. It's healthy. You must finish it all."

I took a sip. It was sweet and warm. I concentrated on swallowing and not being sick.

"The doctor from the island is coming with my boss, Sahmi. Do you need anything?"

I shook my head.

We waited at the table until visiting time at eleven o'clock and then returned to the intensive care corridor. I stepped over the yellow line and into the blue flip-flops. I didn't know what to expect. I crossed the ward to Andrew's bed. He was pale and weak but awake. Relief flooded through me and my eyes filled with tears. I had no idea what they had told him or if he understood.

I sat carefully by the bed and held his hand. "Hello Bubba."

"What's happened?" he asked.

"You're OK," I said, smiling. "It's just been a rough night."

"They said something about my heart," he said, trying to think.

"I don't know," I replied. I was frightened that if I told him it would make his heart rate rise. "It's all alright now."

"Are you alright?"

"I'm fine. I've been here all night, but I'm OK."

His mum, Jenny, rang me, and I passed him the phone.

"We are looking at flights to come out," she said, "but we'll hold off until we know exactly what's happening."

"Don't waste your money," said Andrew. "We'll be back in the resort in a day or so and continuing with our honeymoon. It's really not that serious. I feel absolutely fine now, just a bit tired."

He was so convincing, I believed him.

Visiting on the intensive care ward was only two hours a day, 11am until 12pm and 5pm until 6pm. I put my arms around him and kissed him gently.

"I love you so much," I whispered.

"You too. You've been so brave," he said. "Try and get some rest and we'll head back as soon as we can."

I was still holding him when the alarm on the heart rate monitor began to shriek. Immediately, I panicked. At first I feared I had pressed something. I looked around the room. Andrew's eyes rolled back into his head and he fell against the sheets. A doctor ran to his bed. He grabbed Andrew sharply around the throat. He pressed the artery in his neck forcefully, applying all his weight, Andrew made no noise. I had to stop myself from screaming. Terrified, I watched Andrew's face lose colour and his limbs go limp. His heart rate on the monitor decreased from 190 beats per minute to 80.

"He is stable," said the doctor, "but please, you must leave."

I was terrified. I rang Rob as I walked from the yellow room.

"That sounds positive," he said tentatively. "He was stabilised without being shocked or drugged. It sounds like they have it all under control."

Tholal was sitting on one of the metal corridor chairs. I saw him before he saw me. He was exhausted, his head rested against the wall. He jumped to attention as he heard me approach.

We walked back to the canteen and the foreign office rang. "Paul, our British consul in Malé, will be with you in less than an hour."

We sat and waited until we saw a white man walking confidently across the gravel. He was tall, in his early fifties, clean-shaven and lightly tanned. He wore a Panama hat, white linen shirt, linen shorts and sensible sandals. He shook my hand briskly and acknowledged Tholal. He asked how he pronounced his name, and thanked him for his help. He introduced himself as Paul, in a clear English accent. He pulled a pencil and notepad from his pocket.

"I have been briefed on the situation," he said. "We need to get a handle on what's happening, ensure Andrew gets the best care, and look after your wellbeing." He wrote down each point. "Where are you staying? You need to sleep."

"We were on an island," I said. "We came over last night. I have no luggage, no toiletries, nothing. I just want to stay here."

"You can't stay here, Lauren," he said. "The insurance company will pay for your hotel. The best hotel in Malé is a ten-minute walk away. I advise you stay there. Tholal will take you."

I looked at Tholal. "Of course I will," he said. "We can get you a change of clothes from the town. I will ask our hotel to send over your luggage. It will take a few hours."

"I have contacts at the hospital. I will speak to them," said Paul. He took my number and gave me his. "You have enough money? Do you need anything else?"

"But Andrew," I said, "I can't leave him."

"The nurses won't let you see him again until five," said Tholal. "They have my number if they need you. You must sleep for a few hours."

Paul agreed, and he took his notebook and disappeared inside the hospital.

Tholal and I walked through the hospital and out of the front entrance. The sun was high, and my skin prickled with the heat. He walked to a wall where queues of identical black motorbikes were parked. He surveyed them for a second, trying to find his own. He smiled when he saw it.

"I love my bike," he said proudly.

He straddled the saddle and motioned for me to get on. There was no helmet. It was too hot for helmets. I hesitated, but I had no other choice. My dad would have a fit, I thought – a stranger's motorbike, no helmet and no protective clothes in a place where no one indicates or stops at the traffic lights.

I climbed on the back, clasped my hands around his waist and took a deep breath. We sped down the slope from the hospital to the main road, parallel to the sea. Motorbikes, cars and people filled the streets. I saw whole families crammed onto one bike, older women in headscarves and saris sitting side-saddle, younger women two-handed texting, hardly holding on, businessmen in suits with briefcases making calls.

The roads narrowed with traffic, and we weaved our way round. He didn't stop at junctions. He overtook every bike. He ignored signals and signs, confidently, fluidly, forcing his way though.

He stopped in the town centre and left his bike on the road. I bought a toothbrush, soap, shorts, a T-shirt and underwear from a shop crammed with coloured clothes hung high on the rails.

"Where is the hotel Paul mentioned?" I asked as I got back on the bike, balancing the bags by my feet.

"This way," he said.

We set off again, flying through the streets. Sometimes he turned round to check I was OK. The wind bit my face and tangled my hair; it stung my eyes and caught my breath. I thought of nothing. I found myself smiling unintentionally, and then I wondered how I could smile.

We stopped outside "The best hotel in Malé." It was a stone building painted pink set back from the street. It had glass entrance doors and red stone steps facing the road.

"Thank you," I said. "I enjoyed the ride." And I did.

"I like to see you smile," he said.

The entrance area was small. A flat-screen television hummed on the wall, two leather sofas positioned underneath. There was a gold tiled mosaic in the middle of the white marble floor and a dark reception desk to the side. Neither of the receptionists spoke English. Tholal explained the situation, and the porter took us to see the rooms. The lift was thin and smelt of onions. It was mirrored wall to wall with threadbare carpet underfoot. We slowly ascended to the seventh floor and crossed the corridor. The porter opened the room with a key attached to a large metal card.

"This is the best room," said Tholal smiling happily.

The room smelt of cigarettes, and the carpet was worn. The double bed in the middle of the room was covered with an orange embroidered bedspread. Thick green curtains hung either side of the large wide windows facing the sea. A sailboat bobbed past. A passenger ship sounded its horn. There was a chair in the corner and a dark wooden dresser with drawers that wouldn't open. There was a mirror opposite the bed and a small bedside table with a menu and a phone. The en-suite bathroom was avocado green with a shower over the bath. There were no toiletries in terracotta jars, or thick white towels or champagne flutes.

"It's lovely," I murmured. "I'll take it. It's fine."

The porter handed me the key. I wondered for a second if Tholal would stay. I was scared to be alone.

"I will meet you downstairs just before five to take you for the visiting," he said. "Please try and sleep. I have your number. I will call you in an emergency." He shut the door.

"Thank you," I called after him.

I looked out the window. I lay on the bed. I opened and closed the drawers, checked the lock on the door. I considered the menu, thought I must eat, but couldn't bring myself to order. I watched the clock, but the minutes wouldn't pass. Four hours to visiting. I couldn't sleep. I stood in the shower, washed my hair and scrubbed my skin. I wanted the water to burn me but it was only lukewarm.

I dressed in the new clothes and pulled the comb through my hair. I called my friends on the phone beside the bed. I started to shake. I never stopped shaking.

"Eat some chicken soup," said Emily. "You must keep up your strength."

So I ordered some from the menu and tried to swallow it, but the food stuck in my throat.

"Don't sleep, just rest," said Sarah. I cried until my head hurt and my eyes stung. I pulled the pillow over my head and tried to muffle the image of Andrew falling back on the bed. I clenched my eyes shut and tried to breathe evenly.

Chapter Eight

I must have slept. A shrill noise startled me. I bolted upright, momentarily confused. Where was I? Where was Andrew? Was it the heart rate monitor? Was it a fire alarm? I didn't recognise the noise. I ran clumsily to the door and then saw that the phone beside the bed was ringing. A man with a thick Maldivian accent shouted, "Come downstairs immediately. Very urgent!"

"What's happened?" I spluttered, but the phone went dead.

I scrambled for the key, my phone, my purse. I raced from the room, along the corridor to the lift. I desperately punched the call button and waited for an age. I thought about running down the seven flights of stairs, but every split second I delayed, the lift came closer. I heaved open the doors and cursed as the lift stopped at every floor. I feared the worst. I could hardly breathe. I heard my heart rush in my ears and my teeth chatter. My stomach tensed and my hands felt numb. The lift chimed at the ground floor and I stumbled into the reception.

Standing beside the lift were two men with our suitcases.

"Luggage?" said the taller man in a thick Maldivian accent.

I was shaking and sweating. I could hardly speak.

"Please tell me you just called to say my luggage was here?" I said out of breath.

They looked at one another. They didn't understand.

"Did you call me?" I cried.

They looked at each other again, and then looked at me and shrugged their shoulders. The taller man mimed putting the bags in the lift.

"You scared the shit out of me," I sobbed. "I thought there was

43

something wrong with Andrew."

They smiled and nodded, "Luggage?"

"Yes," I exhaled. "I'll show you to my room."

As I turned towards the lift, Tholal ran across the reception.

"What are you doing?" he shouted. "I called you. I called your phone. I called your mobile. You didn't answer. The hospital rang. We must go there now."

He grabbed my arm. Outside, his motorbike engine was still running. He kicked up the stand. There was a tension in his face that terrified me. He didn't smile. He hardly spoke.

"Is he dead? I asked, but he didn't answer.

"Is he dead?" I cried.

He motioned for me to get onto the bike, and he was pulling away before I had even sat down.

"Please tell me," I sobbed as he weaved his way through the streets.

"I want to hear it from you. Do they want to tell me face to face?" He turned for a second and looked at me.

"Lauren, I don't know. They said it was urgent, very serious."

We stopped at the entrance of the hospital. He threw his bike down on the pavement. He didn't park it carefully or set the stand. I lost my footing and he took my hand. I could hardly walk; my legs wouldn't work. I was shaking uncontrollably. He dragged me through the entrance, pulled me across the floor. Terror and hysteria consumed me. I nearly passed out. The hospital was busy but he pushed people out of the way. He ran up the stairs to the intensive care ward and I followed. He burst into the yellow room and we crossed the line without removing our shoes. He jabbed at the buzzer and hammered on the door. I sat on the bed. I couldn't see straight. I cried and cried. He shouted at the door.

Doctor Latif emerged. I watched how he walked towards us, how he stood, how he held his hands, how he took a deep breath and composed his face.

"Is he dead?" I asked quietly. Tholal gripped my hand.

"Not dead," he said, "but very serious. He had another heart attack. We need to intubate him. He stopped breathing. I need your permission to do this."

"But he's alive? Stable?"

Doctor Latif sat next to me. "Stable, but serious. Your husband will die if we cannot get him to a bigger hospital by the morning. We are only a small hospital, and we are at the limit of what we can do."

"I understand," I said. "I understand, but he is stable, yes?"

"He is critical," said Doctor Latif, "but we have stabilised him."

"Can I see him?" I asked, but he shook his head.

"We need to complete the procedure and then you may see him at five."

Tholal put his arm around me. The yellow walls started to spin; my head throbbed; my stomach convulsed. I ran to the toilet and vomited a mouthful of chicken soup and a litre of coconut juice. He waited for me outside, offered water, a tissue. My throat was raw.

I rang Robert. I wanted him to explain and make sense of it. I didn't understand.

"I've arranged a conference call on Skype with the doctors in Malé and some cardiac specialists from the hospital in Leicester," he said. "The doctors seem to think a virus has attacked and damaged Andrew's heart, but they don't have the equipment to test this fully. From what I understand, they have taken all the right steps."

Tholal took me to pay for the medical procedure. It was two hours until five. We waited in the canteen, sweltering in the bright sun. It burned my skin. I didn't have sunglasses. Tholal handed me his.

"They'll be all the same people at his funeral as at our wedding, just one week later." I started to cry. "Sitting in the same places, dressed in black."

"Don't ever say this," said Tholal. "I won't hear you say this. It is not his time."

I wished I could believe him.

"You must call the insurance people immediately."

"We already know," said the woman from the insurance company. "We are looking for flights. It may be Delhi, Singapore or Bangkok. We need to find the closest, most suitable place. Delhi is the closest, but you will need visas, which may take some time. Bangkok is four hours away but we need to arrange landing permits and secure a medical jet. It may take some days."

"It can't take some days. The doctor said he will die if we don't get him to a better hospital by the morning," I pleaded.

"We are doing our best," said the woman.

"I know you are. I just … I can't … I don't want him to die."

"I appreciate it is an extremely stressful situation. I will call you when I know more."

I leant over the stone wall and watched the people pass. A man walking with his daughter looked up at me and asked if I was OK. I nodded and wiped my eyes. Tholal rose and stood beside me.

"Will you stay with me?" I asked. "I can't do this without you."

"I won't leave you," he said. "I told you before."

Paul, the man from the British consul, arrived a while later. He strolled over to the wall where we were. I explained that Andrew needed to be moved to another hospital urgently. He asked which doctor I had dealt with. Doctor Latif was in the canteen, taking a break. He was sitting on a plastic chair, drinking from a plastic cup with his colleagues. I supposed it was a standard day for him – life and death, all in a day's work. I waved, and he looked up and smiled. Paul went to speak with him. He listened intently as the doctor spoke, making notes with his pencil.

"I'm afraid you're quite right," he said. "It's rather serious now. You must ring the insurers again and ensure they fully understand."

"We cannot arrange a flight for tomorrow morning," the insurance woman said calmly. "It will be the following day at the earliest. We hope to fly you to Bangkok."

"But the doctor said he will die," I sobbed.

"I understand that, but we have problems with landing permits for Malé."

Paul was hopping up and down on the spot, motioning for me to hand him the phone.

"Pass me to your supervisor," he said sharply, "this is not good enough."

He spoke assertively for many minutes, and then ended the call.

"I will speak to the ministers," said Paul. "Don't give up hope. We'll get him a plane. I'll do all I can." He picked up his phone to call his contacts and stepped away from us.

Tholal thought for a moment and picked up his phone too. "My boss, Sahmi, his brother, he works for the airport. He may be able to help with the landing permits."

Sahmi arrived within an hour. He walked into the canteen with the doctor from the resort. He introduced himself and shook my hand firmly. The Doctor's demeanour was different; he looked nervous. He sat down, then stood up again, then paced across the canteen, then spoke with Doctor Latif.

"It's a shock," he said uneasily. "I didn't know."

"You saved his life getting him here."

"There were no signs to suggest it was a problem with his heart. I would have acted earlier."

"I don't blame you."

Sahmi patted The Doctor's arm. They were good friends and had worked together for many years. He was older and stockier than The Doctor. His skin was darker, his hair close cropped. He had also been in the army. As soon as he sat down, his phone began to ring. It was as big as a paperback book, with hundreds of functions, settings and applications. The Doctor made a comment about the size of his own and they laughed a little. Tholal intervened to ask what Sahmi's brother had said.

I sat in the burning heat, mosquitoes biting my legs, the sun scorching my neck, watching strangers around me desperately calling contacts, requesting favours, begging and pleading to save Andrew's life.

"It is resolved," said Sahmi after an hour or so. "The permits are agreed."

"I can confirm that," said Paul.

"Thank you," I said, sobbing.

I called the insurers. "The permits are no longer a problem."

"The plane will be with you in forty-eight hours," she said.

"It needs to be sooner," I stressed. "I have told you before that he will not make it if it takes that long. You said it was a problem with permits. It no longer is."

"This is the information we currently have," she said. "We are doing all we can."

"You clearly aren't," I said, feeling the panic build in my voice. "We have the permits sorted. It's four hours to Bangkok. Why will it take two days?"

"We are investigating every avenue," she said. "If we can get a plane earlier, we will let you know."

"It's money," said Paul. "They must have an upper limit of how much they are able to pay on your policy."

My mind whirred. It made sense. How much was a jet? Could I raise the money? What if Andrew's parents sold their house? What if we asked his brother? What if I asked my family? If we pooled our savings, took out loans, credit cards? Could I raise a million pounds? I knew we could do it. We could raise it. I wouldn't let him die.

I called the insurance company again. "I know it's about money," I said as calmly as I could. "Tell me how much you need and I'll get it."

"It's not about money, Mrs Britton," said the customer service rep. "We need to get the earliest plane to the best possible place and the day after tomorrow is the quickest one we have."

"Of course it's about money," I cried. "Everything's about money. You tell me how much my husband's life is worth, and I will get you that money. I swear, I'll find it, just tell me how much."

"Please Mrs Britton," he said, "you have to believe we are doing everything we can."

I could hardly hear his words, I was crying so hard. If Andrew didn't make it, if I flew home alone, how could I walk into our house? How could I sit in our front room full of unopened wedding presents and unopened cards? How could I sleep in our bed, still unmade on his side? How could I look at the photos from just one week ago?

I returned to the intensive care ward. I knew the way now.

Tholal offered to come with me, but I wanted to walk alone. I sat with Andrew for what I feared would be the last time. He was on a life support machine, a tube down his throat, monitors and wires surrounding the bed. His eyes were closed. His face was grey. Pale blue covers were pulled high around his neck and his feet were covered in an envelope of sheets.

"He hates to have hot feet," I said to a nurse who couldn't understand. "Please make sure his feet stay cool. Please don't cover them up."

I untucked the sheets to show her what I meant. I took his hand. It was limp and lifeless and I held it tight against my cheek. I talked to him. I hoped he could hear. I told him I loved him and he would be OK. I told him about the island, the hotel room, the hospital. I spoke for an hour. I sounded like someone else. I kept my voice light and positive, tried not to stutter or cry. I looked at him for what I feared would be the last time and felt my legs fail. A nurse ran to steady me and led me to a chair. I sat down and took a deep breath. She held my hand.

The doctor from the resort came to speak to the nursing staff. He saw me sitting in the centre of the ward. The nurse said a few words to him and something flashed across his face.

"How do you feel?" he asked, calmly taking my hand from the nurse. "You are very hot. The colour has gone from your skin."

The nurse went to a cupboard and emerged with a thermometer.

"I'm concerned that you may have caught the virus too."

Doctor Latif arrived a few minutes later. He surveyed me carefully and watched the mercury rise. I was shaking violently. I couldn't be sick too. Andrew needed me.

"It's OK," he said warily. "We will keep an eye on you though."

"I don't want to leave him," I whispered.

"We will keep him safe," said Doctor Latif. "You can see him again in the morning. He *will* make it through the night."

Tholal was waiting outside the ward.

"What now?" I said.

"We wait," he replied. "You must eat, and you must rest."

"Come eat with us," said the doctor from the resort, motioning to Sahmi who was still talking on his enormous phone. "We have a table for eight o'clock at the Marble Restaurant. You will like it there."

I looked at Tholal. "Will you come too?"

He turned to his boss, and Sahmi nodded, half-listening, his phone pressed against his ear.

"Then you must sleep," said the hotel doctor. "I am worried about you. You're exhausted."

"There is no way I can sleep," I replied. "I can't stop thinking about Andrew. I can't stop my brain whirring. I'm too scared and stressed to ever sleep again."

"Can't you write her a prescription for some pills?" asked Sahmi, still on his phone.

"I don't know," said The Doctor. "I don't have any paperwork."

"You're a doctor, just do it," said Sahmi.

The Doctor returned with two pills encased in foil.

"It's a bit like Valium, but stronger," he said. "You will definitely sleep."

He handed me the pills and I thanked him. I had no intention of taking them. If Andrew needed me and I didn't wake, I would not forgive myself. I passed them through my fingers in my pocket. The plastic edges were sharp. I would only take them if the worst happened. I prayed I would never take them.

"We have some work to do," said Sahmi. "We will see you at eight."

He spoke intensely to Tholal. I had no idea what he said.

"Let's leave here," said Tholal. "The nurses have my mobile number. They will call if they need you. I will take you around the island before we eat. Try to think about something else."

Chapter Nine

I was too tired to disagree and too weak to think. Tholal and I walked from the front of the hospital, through the reception and out on to the street. His bike, abandoned earlier, obstructed the pavement. He pulled it straight, and I climbed on the back.

"Is it damaged?" I asked.

He smiled and shook his head. "I don't care."

He accelerated swiftly along the long, straight, dusty road beside the sea. We sped over speed bumps and the wheels left the ground. I squeaked a little in excited terror and he turned and smiled.

"I like to make you smile," he said.

The light was beginning to fade. It was quiet beside the ocean. I could see the stones and coral on the sea bed, and the still surf sparkled. Night bathers gathered to swim lengths in the warm clear water. There were floodlit lanes divided by rope, the sexes separated. Women in tunics and headscarves caught their children jumping from the side, serious swimmers overtook others, and men hauled themselves onto the sand. We paused and watched for a while.

"I learnt to swim here," he said.

We rode past large open spaces where political parties preached on huge stages, with primary-coloured banners and bunting hung across the front. Rows of empty chairs faced the platform, and a man stood and shouted into a loudhailer. He pointed his finger and pumped his fists. A scattering of spectators clapped and music blared from a Tannoy.

We stopped at a small park and walked through the tree-lined paths, and then we sat on the swings.

We rode past the palace, the prison, the army barracks – where he had been stationed – the police station, the school. Like a tour guide, he told me stories from each place. We watched learner drivers stutter and stall in a large abandoned car park, driving over bollards and backing into walls. We rode past small food stalls lined up side by side selling hot meats and fizzy drinks, with people crowded around them holding paper cartons and forks. Towers of young coconuts were stacked on the street. Sellers shouted and smiled at customers. It was busy and warm, and the wind rushed past my face.

We stopped by the tsunami monument situated on the sea edge surrounded by a white wall and railings facing the ocean. A tall silver structure stretched to the sky, with vertical iron rods in the centre representing each life lost. Steel balls twisted around the outside. It was peaceful but for the sound of the waves against the rocks below.

"It was 2004 it happened," he said. "There were many lives lost."

"It's so sad," I said. "Did you know any of them?"

He nodded his head. "My family were here. I was in the army abroad. I was so frightened. They survived but I lost some friends."

"I'm sorry. It's a beautiful tribute," I said.

We looked out to sea, leant across the railings, and watched the sun finally set.

"When Andrew is better, you must come back. I will teach you to dive."

"Thank you. I will never forget what you have done for me … for us."

He shrugged his shoulders. "It's just my job."

We returned to his bike and I jumped as his phone rang. I searched his face for a sign. He looked serious. He listened, and he seemed to say he understood.

"It was Sahmi," he said calmly. "Andrew is stable. He wants me to return to the hotel resort this evening. He has work he needs me to do. He can't let me stay."

"But, you can't leave me," I said quietly. "You are my only friend. You are the only person who understands. I can't do this without you."

He shook his head. "What can I do? He is my boss. I must do what he tells me."

"I will talk to him," I said. "He might take pity on me."

"Maybe you can speak to him at the restaurant."

The Marble Restaurant was at the top of a tall building, uncovered in the evening air, with a low wall around the edge that faced the great expanse of sea. The light was fading; street lamps and boat headlights were illuminated in the water. It was busy, people sitting around long black tables, while waiters attended them with trays of drinks.

The Doctor sat at the table with Sahmi and a woman I didn't recognise. They had large cocktail glasses of coloured liquid in front of them. They chatted easily and laughed at something The Doctor said. The woman was his fiancée. They were due to marry in two weeks' time. She was beautiful, with delicate features, large brown eyes, long dark eyelashes and thick glossy hair. Her dimples showed when she smiled and she smiled often as she watched the doctor speak.

"I am so sorry about what has happened," she said, grasping my hand. "If there is anything I can do, please ask. It must be terrible for you."

She worked on another resort. She had met The Doctor when she had been unwell.

"She was unwell a lot after that," joked Sahmi.

Tholal sat awkwardly beside his boss. I ordered food I couldn't eat, sipped a fruit juice and felt the acidity burn my throat.

"Please just eat this," whispered Tholal, pushing a slice of pizza towards me. I chewed and chewed but I couldn't swallow. The bread swelled in my mouth and my stomach groaned. I willed myself to finish and not to be sick.

Tholal went to the bar and I took my chance.

"Sahmi," I said carefully, "can Tholal support me tomorrow and not go back to the resort? He is the only person I trust, the only person who understands."

The Doctor laughed. "Hey! What about us?"

I smiled. "You have both been amazing, but Tholal has been there from the start."

Sahmi thought for second. "If that is what you want," he said.

I smiled and nodded, and he went and spoke to Tholal at the bar.

The light faded and the food was finished. Sahmi ate mine. Tholal walked me back to my room. "What time in the morning should I get you?" he asked.

"I won't sleep, so anytime, but *you* need to rest."

"I'll be in the reception at nine," he said, leaving, and I watched him walk away.

Fraser, Andrew's father, rang as I shut the door.

"Good news, Lauren," he said, "I think Rob told you he'd arranged a telephone case conference with the hospital doctors and his friend from the university – a cardiac specialist. They have spoken about Andrew's condition. It looks like a virus. The heart isn't permanently damaged. It will be easy to sort. He has also spoken to the insurance company, and they may have a flight to Bangkok for tomorrow afternoon. They will call to confirm. Jenny and I are booking flights now."

I put the pills from the doctor on the bedside table. I noticed our suitcases had been delivered and were placed on the floor..

I opened my bag and Andrew's T-shirts and books fell out. I shivered with shock and sadness. I'd expected my items in my bag and Andrew's in his. I couldn't touch his things. The clothes he had happily packed, the books he chose at the airport, his sun cream, his sun hat, his flip-flops, his shorts. I started to cry. I sobbed uncontrollably and my whole body shook. I knelt on the floor surrounded by his stuff and couldn't breathe. I remembered his ring on the side. I wondered where it would be. I couldn't search through the luggage. I felt a physical pain.

I couldn't sleep. All night I paced around the room. I sat down, stood up, laid down, closed my eyes, thought of Andrew and cried. I rang my friends, my family, Andrew's mum and dad. I watched the clock, watched the boats and jumped every time my phone rang. As nine o'clock neared, I showered, dressed in the shorts and shirt and walked down the seven flights of stairs to meet Tholal in the foyer.

I didn't recognise him immediately. He was wearing a bright purple shirt. I was looking for him in his uniform. He didn't see me either until I stood right in front of him.

"You look different, better," he said.

"You too," I replied. "Did you get some sleep?"

He nodded.

"Have you spoken to the hospital?" I asked.

"He's fine," he said. "I checked every hour."

I smiled. "Thank you, but every hour? You couldn't have slept."

He waved my comment away. "Don't worry about me."

"When can I see him?"

"Visiting time is at eleven. Do you want to ride until then?"

We walked out of the entrance and I climbed onto the back of his motorcycle.

We rode the opposite way this time and I saw the sights in the light. We sat at the monument again and he passed me a pastry. I pretended to eat.

"What are these?" he asked, pointing to the red welts on my legs.

"Mosquito bites," I replied.

"I'll kill them all," he said seriously, turning back to the sea.

"What will people think, a white woman on the back of your bike? I said.

"I don't care what people think. I will do anything for you."

Chapter Ten

The insurance company called just before ten. "We have a flight for four o'clock to Bangkok. We have a contact in Malé who will liaise with the hospital and arrange all the logistics. We'll be in touch."

We sat and waited in the canteen. Sahmi, The Doctor, the general manager of the resort and an Australian named Chris arrived. He was tall and thin, casually dressed in shorts and a white shirt. His face was flushed with worry, and he made nervous phone calls, asked about Andrew, checked on me, checked his watch, spoke to the nursing staff, stood up, sat down. He was anxious that the transfer went smoothly.

As soon as I said anything, he was on the phone straight away. "Tissues, we need tissues. Get Lauren a multipack. Mosquito bites, she's got mosquito bites. Somebody find some spray. How's the light? Is it too bright? Do you need sunglasses? Can we get you sunglasses? Have you eaten? Do you need food?"

Our bags were still packed in my hotel room, and he sent a man to collect them.

I visited Andrew at eleven o'clock. I held his hand. He was still sedated with a tube from his throat and wires from his arms. His feet were uncovered as I had requested. His skin was grey. The nurses smiled encouragingly and Doctor Latif was positive.

"As soon as he gets to Bangkok, he will be OK."

I signed pieces of paperwork and handed over my credit card. I went with Tholal to buy supplies directed by the hospital. I bought sheets and pillows for the flight, water and medicine, a dressing gown, a buttoned shirt for easy access, and liquid food. He negotiated the price in the shops. I carried the goods on the back of his bike, my arms laden. Then we waited as before.

"The flight is due to land earlier than expected," said the insurance company. "A medical team from Thailand will arrive at the airport at 3pm. They will arrive by ambulance at the hospital where they will then transport Andrew by ambulance back to the airport and on to the plane. The flight is four hours to Bangkok and then twenty minutes to Bangkok Heart Hospital."

I relayed this to the team around me.

"They do know they can't get an ambulance to the airport?" said Tholal. "The airport is on an island. You can only get there by boat."

"I'll call them," said Sahmi.

I heard him try to explain, and then speak uneasily to Chris, who took over the phone.

"It's absolutely fine," said Chris. "We will use one of our boats if we have to. Please don't worry at all."

We returned to the intensive care corridor and the row of chairs. A little girl sitting next to me was playing a hand-held computer game. She showed me the screen and the magic coins she was collecting. I stopped thinking about Andrew and detached from everything. I felt I was looking in on somebody else from above. Tholal sat on my other side. He held his head in his hands.

Robert rang again. "We'll come if you need us. Mum and Dad are on their way," he said. "An old friend from university, Paul, lives in Bangkok. I've spoken to him. He'll come and meet you at the hospital, so you're not on your own. I'll text you his number. I've given him yours. He's a very good friend. He'll look after you until our parents get there."

"OK," I said. But I had hardly heard.

"I have contacted my colleague, the general manager of our hotel in Bangkok," said Chris, who was anxiously checking his phone. "His name is Markus. He will look after you. The company will pay for your room. I have told them which hospital Andrew is going to, and they will pick you up when you arrive."

"OK," I said, unable to process the information.

The Thai team arrived and were ushered immediately into the intensive care ward. I followed them and hovered by the nurses' station. There was a doctor with a large backpack, a young male nurse, a female nurse with short hair and a lady with a camera hung around her neck clutching a clipboard. They wore matching white, collared T-shirts.

They spent a long time examining Andrew, and they spoke to Doctor Latif at length. They calmly and efficiently set up the mobile medical equipment to enable Andrew to be moved. Finally, they escorted his bed from the room while the lady with the camera took photographs.

I didn't get a chance to thank Doctor Latif. He had saved Andrew's life. I looked for him desperately, but we had to move. I hugged the nurses.

I followed behind the stretcher – the machines and monitors flashing and beeping – down the corridor and outside to where the ambulance was parked. Tholal and Sahmi helped the paramedics load Andrew inside. I couldn't travel in the ambulance as there wasn't enough space; the Thai team sat beside him. A taxi arrived to take Chris, The Doctor and Sahmi and I to the port where we would take a ferry to the airport.

"What about you?" I asked Tholal.

"I'll ride. I'll get there quicker. I need to help at the other end."

"I want to come with you."

"Stay with the others. Please."

I watched him ride away, speeding after the ambulance.

The ferry port was bustling, it was market day. It smelt of fish and food. There were hundreds of people crowded around the dock. Tourists climbed on and off the boats, struggling with their bags; traders with boxes transported their goods; workers and ferry staff moved swiftly through the throng. Motorbikes beeped and cars came to a standstill. Buggies and children, old people and animals walked and jostled up the high stone sides from the pavement to the sea edge.

There were maybe ten wide white boats, with a cargo area at the front and staggered seating behind with small white chairs and leather-covered cushions shaded by a thin plastic sheet. The seats were still wet from the spray.

Sahmi jumped from the taxi and spoke to a ferry driver who nodded that he understood. I looked for Tholal. The paramedics considered how to move Andrew from the ambulance and onto the boat. There was no clear path, and there were people everywhere. I couldn't see Tholal. Sahmi shouted something and suddenly he was there ushering people back. The men lifted the stretcher from the ambulance and passed Andrew across the crowd, people raising their hands to steady him, strangers helping to ease the bed onto the boat. The Thai team carried the equipment carefully. Regular passengers followed behind. The photographer caught these moments. It was entirely surreal.

I sat on a plastic seat, and my phone wouldn't work. Andrew was strapped to the stretcher, unconscious with tubes down his throat. Sahmi, The Doctor, Tholal and Chris held each corner of the bed. The ferry started, and the bed began to slide. Strangers stood up swiftly to steady the stretcher.

Tholal gripped the mattress with both hands. There were eight people around the bed now, holding it down. Waves crashed either side of the boat and it rocked violently. He caught my eye and smiled weakly.

The journey took fifteen minutes, and I remembered the airport island a little from a few days earlier. They carried Andrew on the stretcher from the boat and pushed the bed through the cargo entrance of departures. I followed the others through the clear wide corridors and clutched our passports and presented them when asked.

We paused at the final departure door, and the officials checked my passport one last time. There was a small jet on the runway in the distance. I shook Chris's hand, hugged Sahmi and The Doctor. Tholal was wearing his sunglasses, although it was dark inside.

"Be safe," he said casually, holding his hand out to shake.

I ignored it and hugged him tightly, tried to stop myself from crying. "Thank you so much. Thank you for everything. I will never forget what you have done for us. Thank you with all my heart. Thank you, thank you."

"You are so strong," he said, handing me a small slip of paper. "This is my phone number and my email address. Please let me know when you get to Bangkok. Please let me know how Andrew is."

I folded the paper and carefully placed it in my pocket. "Of course I will. I promise."

I followed the Thai team and the aircrew onto the runway and turned back for a second to wave goodbye. I saw him wipe his eyes under his glasses and turn back to the hall.

Chapter Eleven

The Maldivian aircrew lifted Andrew onto an empty shuttle bus. The Thai team followed, inspecting the monitors, holding the drips high, photographing everything. The heat was unbearable. Condensation steamed the windows, and sweat dripped from everyone's faces. Andrew, sedated, sleepily opened his eyes. He blinked a little and stared at me.

"He hates to be too hot," I said to no one. I was worried about the heat. His face was red. I didn't want him to become distressed. "He hates to be too hot," I said again. I swear I saw him nod. I waved my passport above him, furiously fanning the air.

We stopped in front of the jet and they moved him off of the bus. It was just as hot outside. I was sticky and stressed, and my heart was hammering in my chest. I felt sick and weak.

The captain pulled down a ramp from inside the jet. The aircrew and the Thai team heaved to push him inside. I stood back and watched, until they beckoned me on board. It was small inside with dark oak veneer trimmings, like the interior of a posh car, and soft brown leather seats. There were champagne glass holders in the armrests, and flat-screen TVs. The stretcher filled the space along the far side, and there were monitors and oxygen tanks fixed to the wall. Opposite were two seats facing each other. The two nurses sat there, observing the screens. Behind them sat the Thai doctor, calmly tapping on his laptop. At Andrew's feet was a small sofa where the photographer was sitting. She motioned for me to sit next to her and I nervously sat down. The captain was Australian.

"We're good to go," he said, smiling, and returned to the cockpit.

The air conditioning blasted. It was freezing cold. I shivered with fear, and my teeth chattered with cold. The photographer smiled and pulled a blanket from under the seat. The male nurse said something and they all laughed.

"He said that Europeans are always cold," translated the photographer.

I smiled a little. "I am."

I pulled the blankets around me, and the photographer explained the plan. We would be met at Bangkok airport and travel to the best heart hospital in Thailand.

"It is the king's hospital, where he goes," she said.

"They treated me there last year," said the Thai doctor. "I had electrics problems with my heart. They gave me a small operation and I am fine now. It will be the same for your husband."

I nodded and tried to settle into the seat. I signed a disclaimer for if Andrew did not survive.

The television displayed four hours to arrival, a cartoon image of our plane over the Maldives inching across the screen. I looked at Andrew – he was sleeping peacefully – but as I watched him, I became aware of smoke rising around the bottom of the bed. The monitors began to alarm. I looked to the photographer, panicked.

"Smoke!" I cried, pointing. "What's wrong? What's going on?"

The nurses stood, and the doctor looked up from his laptop. They checked the equipment, adjusted a wire and spoke to the doctor. I watched as he smiled.

"The air conditioning is cold and the oxygen tanks are warm," he said, laughing. "Steam has been created."

I breathed again. "I thought his bed might explode."

They looked at me, not understanding, smiled and nodded again.

The photographer offered me soft drinks, water and some food in a cool box. I chose a small sushi pack and picked at the rice. I swallowed a mouthful and it stuck in my throat. The rest of them chatted calmly.

I watched the minutes to landing slowly decrease. I watched Andrew's chest move. I jumped every time the monitor bleeped. I tried to stay calm. I imagined his parents boarding the plane to

Bangkok, not knowing if he was still alive. I shivered under the blankets and the photographer gave me her coat. I worried he wouldn't make it. I worried about the landing, the change in air pressure, the size of the plane. After four long hours we touched down smoothly and the jet ground to a halt.

An aircrew opened the doors and pulled down the metal ramp. They manoeuvred Andrew from the plane and into an ambulance waiting on the tarmac. There were people surrounding us: men and women in smart white tunics embroidered with the hospital emblem, air officials in navy suits and hats, transport police, customs officers, porters and ambulance drivers. There were so many people, each one smartly dressed, each one performing their part with perfect precision.

The runway was floodlit. It was nine o'clock at night but as warm as day. There were low airport buildings in the distance, and I could hear the sound of planes taking off. We had made it to Bangkok and Andrew was alive.

Part Two

Chapter Twelve

I sat at the front of the ambulance. I could see Andrew in the back through a gap in the seats, lying on the stretcher. His eyes were closed.

I called Robert to tell him we had safely arrived.

I texted Tholal, "We made it." I felt lost without him.

I called Robert's friend in Bangkok, Paul.

"I'll meet you at the hospital. I'll find you there," he said in a strong Irish accent.

The sirens screamed. We sped across the runway and through the tall sentried gates. I watched as the guards saluted. We drove out onto the freeway. Huge wide roads overlapped each other like a Scalextric track. There were cars in every lane, respectfully overtaking, stopping at toll points and avoiding the masses of motorcycle taxis. Soaring skyscrapers crowded the skyline. Tall illuminated buildings, high-rise flats, hotels and offices with hundreds of floors lit up the city. Enormous billboards advertising cars and fizzy drinks, in English and Thai, reached out on to the road, obscuring the windows of the apartments behind.

At the lower level, houses were crowded together. Shacks with corrugated iron roofs, unstable lean-tos and makeshift homes with satellite dishes balanced on top. Large stray dogs slept beneath the underpass by the road. Street food displayed on trestle tables was sold in shacks structured from iron poles, held together with plastic sheets and cardboard. Sellers sold unidentifiable meat on skewers, throwing tiny titbits to the dogs. They stirred large cooking pots of soups, and sliced up bright yellow plastic-textured mango-like fruit.

As we turned off the freeway, wealth and poverty existed side by side. A large glass-fronted showroom with hundred-thousand-pound cars was located next to a shack shop fixing tyres. A fat man sat shirtless, cross-legged like a Buddha, his tummy spilling over his shorts and his family around him on newspapers and oil-covered sheets. His wife was holding a baby, food packets on the floor. We passed brightly lit newsagents and large warehouse buildings, wedding dress shops with beautiful expensive white dresses in the window and filthy street sellers in front, their shoeless feet dirty and dusty, tending piles of magazines or T-shirts displayed on cardboard boxes. Luminous pink flashing signs for adult entertainment peaked over walls. On some street corners and by the sides of the roads, small stone shrines stood with yellow flowers around the statues. Brightly lit photographs of the king in golden frames hung from the sides of buildings and beside certain shrines. He was pictured sitting on his throne with his dog at his feet.

The largest picture of the king was at the entrance to the hospital. It was a huge framed painting on a white stone plinth. The ambulance followed blue and red signs to "Bangkok Heart Hospital". We turned from the main road and across a railway track. Motorcycle taxi drivers in bright orange vests congregated under the bridge. Rows of shacks selling food filled the sides of the streets. The roads were potholed and unmade and the ambulance bounced over the cracks. We passed a restaurant with shisha pipes outside, a smart Arab hotel, a row of red-brick shops, a hair salon, a small glass-fronted three-storey shopping mall – the "Bangkok Plaza" – with Starbucks signs flashing through the ground-floor window.

The hospital was suddenly in front of me. A great white building, three sides of a hollow square, floors and floors of wide windows like an enormous Majorcan holiday hotel. A statue of the god Garuda was suspended above the hospital sign. The image of the god was a strong man with an eagle's beak and wings outstretched in gold and red, watching above the entrance. There was a large shrine in the middle. It was a raised white marble area. Floodlit, glowing in the darkness, and there were two large candles burning within large metal lanterns. There was a kneeling stone and an altar directly in front of the shrine. The shrine was covered with flowers, opened fizzy drinks with straws poking out, baskets of eggs, sweets and fruit. Behind the first shrine, another was under construction. Two grey stone elephants rose up from the rubble, and they wore stethoscopes around their necks. Ambulances, cars and motorbikes pulled in and out of the area, directed by uniformed officials in smart hats and white gloves.

Relatives waited patiently for bright pink taxis to pull up next to the shrine. Nurses in knee-length skirts, tunic tops, and small caps pinned to their heads, dressed in pastel colours and sensible flat shoes, daintily climbed side-saddle onto waiting motorbike taxis and sped off into the night.

A female traffic warden guided the ambulance into a holding bay directly outside the foyer. I stepped down from the seat and she saluted. I nearly saluted back. Nurses, doctors and porters had already arrived. All were smartly dressed in immaculate uniforms, and they took no time at all to move the bed where Andrew was strapped, unconscious, from the ambulance and into the hospital.

I watched as a large black limousine pulled up outside the entrance. An attractive young Thai lady stepped out and towards me. She had long black hair and a beautiful smile. She wore a pleated grey skirt, high heels, a tailored black jacket and a smart white blouse. She approached me.

"Mrs Britton?" she asked.

"Yes," I said uncertainly.

"My name is Tu. Markus, the manager at the Intercontinental Hotel, has sent me to look after you. I will stay with you to speak to the doctors and translate for you. Then when Mr Britton is settled, I will take you back to the hotel. Your luggage has already been collected from the airport."

Our luggage. I had forgotten that we ever had any.

"Thank you so much," I said.

She smiled and took my hand. We followed the Thai team inside. I nearly called Robert's friend Paul to tell him not to come. I felt entirely confident and reassured.

The hospital air conditioning hit me as I walked through the automatic doors. The floor was bright white polished marble, without footprints or scuffs. An illuminated heart three metres high, with red lights like blood travelling through the ventricles, was situated in the centre. Flat-screen televisions flashed on the white walls. There was pristine red leather seating positioned in front. A large reception desk was stationed at the end. Fixed to the wall was a board of photographs of the doctors like a "Guess Who" game, organised in order, the most important person at the top. The signs were in English and Thai.

We waited for the lift. The porters pushed Andrew in first, and the nurses and doctors followed. Tu and I waited for the next lift. She pressed the button for the third floor, "Immediate Cardiac Care". The doors opened into a waiting area with more white marble flooring and large comfortable sofas positioned in a square. There were vases of fresh flowers on the coffee table, magazines and a water dispenser. A Thai couple waited calmly for news of a relative, their bags by their feet. At the end of the area were frosted glass doors concealing the ward.

A nurse came out and spoke to Tu.

"We'll wait here until he is settled, then you can see him, then we'll return to the hotel," she said, still smiling and sitting down next to me.

"Thank you," I said. "How long do you think?"

"Maybe an hour," she replied. "Have you eaten?"

I shook my head.

"I will get you some food."

I waited for a few minutes, and then a smartly dressed nurse, her hair tied in a low bun with a small cap pinned to her head, motioned for me to come through. She sat me down in the centre of the room where there were a group of desks with eight computer screens, all representing the glass-fronted rooms made up with white sheets and eight flat-screen televisions. The high-tech equipment in each room looked barely used. There were eight cardiac patients and eight female nurses clutching folders of paper, urine bottles and drips.

A young male doctor in a long white lab coat approached me. He was short, with a thick fringe and glasses. He asked me a lot of questions but did not seem to entirely understand my answers. I spoke slowly and clearly, and I tried to explain. He asked me about Andrew's allergies, previous health problems, if he was a drug addict and what had happened in Malé. He nodded, wrote words on a clipboard, consulted charts and X-rays and then asked me the same questions again.

"He will be OK?" I asked.

The doctor looked at me carefully. "There is nothing more we can do for him," he said.

I had not expected his response. "I'm sorry," I said, standing. "I don't understand."

"There is nothing we can do for him," he said again. "His heart is only working at ten per cent."

The air conditioning was freezing, and my head began to spin. I was tired, so tired. I hadn't slept for days. I felt sick and starving. I heard bleeps and alarms, words I couldn't understand. I smelt disinfectant, cleaning fluids, floor polish. My knees began to buckle. I felt cold clean marble against my face.

"Lauren, I'm Paul." I heard an Irish voice. He held out his hand and helped me to my feet. He was Robert's age, thirty-five, with serious eyes and dark hair greying at the temples.

"What's happening?" he asked, guiding me to a chair.

"Please talk to them," I said, my teeth chattering in fear and shock. I could hardly form a sentence.

"They ... they ... they said there is nothing ... nothing ... there is nothing they can do ... nothing they can do for Andrew." Tears were streaming down my face. "What do I do now? I need to see him. I need to see him. We came all this way."

"My wife is Thai," he said. "I speak the language a little, I understand well. I will speak to the doctor. Please just sit here for a second. I will sort this out."

They spoke in hushed tones, although I couldn't understand. Paul nodded, clenched his fists, and then pressed his palms to the side of his head. He took a few steps towards me. I took a deep breath.

"What did he say?" I asked. "What did he say?"

"It's the first night, they need to stabilise him more. His heart is not in a good way."

"Is there nothing they can do for him?"

"I think … I think you should try and sleep. Where are you staying? Do you have somewhere? You are welcome to stay at our house. We can come back in the morning with my wife. She can speak to them clearly."

I knew he had heard the same as me.

"Thank you, but my bags are at the hotel, just ten minutes from here. They sent a lady to get me, and I should probably go there."

Tu returned, smiling, holding a Starbucks bag. She pulled a sandwich and a cake from the brown paper packaging.

"For you," she said.

Paul spoke to her. "Please take Lauren back," he said. "She is not in a good way."

"I want to see Andrew," I whispered.

The nurse showed me into his room, and Paul followed me. As before, there were monitors above his head, drips in his arms, and tubes down his throat. He looked like he was sleeping.

"I met Andrew a few times in Manchester," Paul said, "when Rob and I were at university. He's a really good guy."

"Will you tell Rob?" I said, suddenly remembering the family. "I can't tell him. How can I tell them? How can I tell them? I can't tell them. I can't tell them."

"Of course," said Paul.

I stroked Andrew's hand.

"You're going to be OK, Bubby. It's all going to be OK."

He didn't stir. I cried quietly beside his bed. I tried to think of the right words to say goodbye. I feared it would be the last time I ever saw him. I tried to take in all of Andrew's face. I remembered him smiling at me on our wedding day as I walked down the aisle, and us laughing, holding hands and repeating our vows, and bed swimming, and watching *Merlin* and walking across the common. This couldn't be the last time I saw him alive. I kissed his head. I was shaking so hard I was almost convulsing. I breathed in gasps. The nurses gathered outside the room.

"We have to go," said Tu, helping me to my feet and out of the room. "This is the best hospital in Thailand. They *will* help him, I promise."

Paul returned home and Skyped Rob from his kitchen. He later told me that it was the hardest phone call he had ever made. His three children were sleeping upstairs. He tried to hold himself together, but he was pale and shaking. He tried not to cry. His wife stood behind him, and he held his head in his hands.

"I don't know how to tell you this, mate."

Rob booked flights to Bangkok the second the call ended. He needed to be beside his brother. He was terrified that he wouldn't see him again. His parents were already in the air.

Chapter Thirteen

Tu and I descended in the hospital lift. I leant against the side. A black limousine pulled up outside, and the driver opened the door. There was a bottle of water and tissues in the footwell. Tu handed me both. I felt like I was looking from above at another person. This wasn't me; this wasn't my life.

We travelled from the hospital, across the freeway, along the central shopping streets. We drove beside the sky rail. High above us, the trains rushed past as commuters climbed the sets of steps. We sped past enormous department stores illuminated with extravagant Christmas decorations, enormous coloured globes stretched between street lamps like giants' fairy lights. Twinkling stars, glittering lanterns and huge wrapped boxes of presents hung from the wires above. Sparkling Christmas trees filled the pavements, massive moving reindeer, and gingerbread men standing to attention. Tourists and residents sidestepped through waving snowmen, and smiling snow monkeys, thick scarves wound around their necks. They negotiated past gigantic Ferrero Rocher pyramids and a Santa's hut. There was fake snow covering the floor and fake ice and icicles in the sweltering heat.

Late at night the central streets buzzed. We passed stalls selling meats and fruits, T-shirts and books. We passed tourists, families, couples and children. It could have been morning rush hour, and the traffic swelled. Bright pink taxis, brightly coloured rickshaws, motorbikes and bicycles all fought through the throng. The limousine cruised along. I pressed my nose to the glass and thought of nothing.

We turned right into the hotel entrance. The Intercontinental stood thirty-seven storeys high. It was a silver and blue curved building, with hundreds of windows, great panes of glass, beautiful fountains in the driveway and cultivated trees. There was a statue of Garuda where limousines queued in a line. There were several steps to the entrance, where porters stood in smart brown collarless suits. They opened the doors and bowed, palms pressed together. There was one tall porter, his trouser bottoms flapping around his ankles, his sleeves a little too short. He reminded me of a Beatles album cover, his hair the same style. He smiled genuinely, and bowed awkwardly. I followed Tu through to the reception desk.

The foyer was vast and elegant, but supersized. The floor was cream-coloured stone polished brightly, and a huge majestic staircase curved down from the mezzanine floor. Great pillars stretched to the ceiling fifty feet above and glass walls looked out onto Bangkok. There was a circular seating area with an enormous festive floral display featuring tall red, gold and green flowers. A beautifully lit Christmas tree taller than Trafalgar Square's was situated in the corner. Behind, there were steps down to a piano bar with dark purple velvet chairs and a grand piano set in the middle. Customers sat at low, dark wood tables facing the bar, the spirit bottles backlit, the ice sculptures glistening. To the right of this was the concierge desk, lifts, more seating, stairs and escalators.

The receptionists were dressed the same as Tu. She located my key and led me to my room. We ascended thirty floors, and a man – his sole job to call for the lift – bowed as we stepped in. He pressed the buttons and stepped back to greet the next guest.

"The swimming pool is on the roof," she said. "The spa and gym are on the thirty-first floor, you are invited to breakfast in the club lounge on the thirty-third floor, and we serve afternoon tea at two and cocktails and canapés from five. Please call if you need anything. Please try to sleep. He will be safe."

I swiped the card, thanked Tu, and stepped into the room. The bed was king-sized; a note on the pillow welcomed me to the hotel and offered me a pillow menu with twenty-seven options. It made my head hurt. There was a huge sideboard, a 38-inch flat-screen television, a chaise longue, a desk and chair, a huge vase of fresh flowers and an entirely marble bathroom with beautifully packaged toiletries. There were complimentary bottles of water by the bed, chocolates, and a list of spa treatments. The windows looked out high across the city, all lit up at night. I sat on the windowsill. I tried not to be sick.

Tholal replied to my text.

"I am so happy you are there. I am so happy that Andrew will now be getting better. I said it wasn't his time."

I didn't tell him. I couldn't communicate the pain I felt.

I stood in the shower and then dressed in the same clothes I had worn all day. I couldn't face sorting through my luggage. Andrew's clothes were still mixed up with mine. I read and re-read the pillow menu. I took the lift to the roof and leant over the side. I pulled open a sun lounger and sat on the edge. I watched the water shimmer in the swimming pool. I wandered the corridors like a ghost.

I returned to the room and lay on the bed, turned the lights off, turned them on. I turned the air conditioning up and then down again. I could not turn on the television; it felt wrong. I tried to sleep, but sleep wouldn't come. I feared my phone would ring, that the hospital would call. I jumped at every sound, every footstep in the corridor, every door that slammed shut.

I stopped crying for a second and then it hit me again, like the first time.

"There is nothing we can do. Nothing we can do. Nothing."

The phone rang. It startled me. I was reminded of the Tannoy. My breath caught in my throat.

"Iain and I are coming to Bangkok," said my dad. "Mum is staying with your sister and George. We can't stand the thought of you being alone. We'll be there tomorrow afternoon. It *will* be OK."

I felt the tears fall down my face again. My family don't like travelling far from home. I understood my dad was facing his worst fears to be with me and the fact caught in my throat.

"This means a lot. Thank you. Thank you so much."

"We love you, Lauren." I heard his voice break. "You must be so scared, but keep strong for just a few more hours and we'll be there."

"I'll try," I whispered, desperate to feel the security of home.

I waited until the sun began to rise between the skyscrapers. The city in the early morning had a slightly grey tinge from the thick smog rising from the traffic below. From my window I saw tall glass buildings, hotels, office blocks, storeys and storeys of them, like upright dominos, far into the distance. I tried to find the hospital, squinted to see the sign. I picked out a large green golf course, the railway and pink taxis like toy cars from the thirtieth floor. I felt an aching terror in my stomach, and I could hardly breathe. Andrew's parents were due to arrive that morning, but I couldn't remember when. I needed to see them. I felt entirely alone.

I inspected my face in the bathroom mirror. I had never looked so unwell. My skin was thick with spots, greasy and pale. My eyes were red and swollen, and my lips bled from biting them. I found some make-up in my handbag and rubbed it roughly into my cheeks. It didn't make a difference. I turned off the light.

Chapter Fourteen

I walked to breakfast on the thirty-third floor and was greeted by the receptionist, Julia, a beautiful German girl with clear white porcelain skin. She smiled warmly and took me to a table, brought me a mug of hot water and encouraged me to eat. I observed the businessmen filling their plates from the breakfast buffet, tapping at their laptops, turning their newspaper pages. I ate a corner of a pancake.

"A car and a translator will be waiting for you in the foyer at half past nine to take you to the hospital. Your parents-in-law have just arrived," said Julia.

"Thank you," I said jumping from my seat, rushing to the lift.

Jenny and Fraser were sitting under the Christmas tree. They looked tired and small, their faces strained with stress, their eyes ringed red with fatigue.

They saw me across the foyer, and stood shakily. They walked towards me, overwhelmed. I felt relief in my chest and a weight rise from my shoulders. I couldn't cry.

They hugged me hard.

"You've done so well," Jenny said. "We're here now. It's alright. We're here now."

"The hotel staff met us at the airport," said Fraser. "They rushed us through, and they told us Andrew got here OK. It's the best heart hospital in Thailand. We were so relieved. We were on the flight for fifteen hours, not knowing if he had made it alive."

He hugged me tightly. "It's OK, kid."

They hadn't spoken to Rob. I didn't tell them what had happened at the hospital.

A tall, well-dressed man approached us as we waited for the car.

"I am Markus, the general manager," he said, extending his hand. We later learnt he was Swiss. His English was perfect. He wore a perfectly tailored dark grey suit, perfectly ironed shirt and perfect shiny shoes. His short blonde hair was combed neatly, and his teeth shone bright white.

"I wish to express my sadness at the situation you find yourselves in. If there is anything we can do to support you, please let either myself or my staff know. Your rooms are complimentary. The food, the cars to the hospital – they will not be charged. I will send someone to translate for you each day. But please do not hesitate to ask for anything else you require."

He went to shake my hand, and I read the situation wrong. I launched into an awkward hug, leaving an imprint of foundation on the shoulder of his suit. He didn't flinch at the uncomfortable embrace.

"This is Nat, the customer service manager. She will accompany you today," he said, introducing the tall beautiful Thai girl standing by his side. She was smartly dressed in a blazer and knee-length skirt and low leather heels. She had long dark hair and dark oval eyes. She wore small Chanel earrings and a silver watch sparkled on her wrist.

"Very nice to meet you," she said in English with the hint of an Australian accent. I discovered later that she had lived in Sydney for many years. She signalled to the door porters. A car pulled up instantly and she led us outside.

She stepped into the front seat, spoke to the driver quickly, and nodded. She directed the car to the hospital, explaining the quickest route while tapping on her Blackberry and maintaining her conversation with us.

The driver drove calmly through the chaotic traffic, merging between oncoming cars and negotiating past motorbikes. In the daylight it was busier, bustling, and intense. I counted the stray dogs by the side of the street – twelve – and tried to stop thinking about Andrew. I tried to prepare myself for the worst. I should have told his parents, but they seemed so positive.

The same traffic warden as yesterday beckoned the car into the hospital. Nat opened the door and strode ahead. She spoke to the staff on the ground floor and led us to the lift. My stomach lurched. My knees felt week. I swallowed my nerves. I heard Jenny take a deep breath and Fraser reached for her hand. The lighted floor numbers ascended, and the lift spoke to us in English "second floor". I tried to move out into the waiting area where we had begun last night, but my legs would not carry me. It took all my strength to pass through the closing lift doors, to take the few steps forward, to walk towards the ward.

I let his parents enter first. I hovered behind and sat on the sofas. The couple I had seen yesterday had spent the night there. They had pushed the chairs together to form a bed; she was dressed in pyjamas, and he looked only half-awake. They took their toothbrushes to the toilet. I was grateful we had somewhere to stay.

Nat approached the doctors, and Jenny and Fraser crowded round. I hung back. Doctor Don Pichet was introduced as Andrew's lead doctor. The doctor I had seen the night before was not on shift. Doctor Don was taller than the other doctors, in his mid-forties, with slightly greying hair. He was occasionally unshaven when he had worked all night and he blinked furiously when he was nervous or had to deliver bad news. As time went on I began to scrutinise his blinking for clues. He explained that Andrew's heart function was very low because his heart had swollen as a result of the virus. His English was reasonable but he didn't always understand.

"The doctor, yesterday, he said there was nothing you could do for him," I blurted out.

"Yes," he said, "nothing we could do for him last night, specialist surgeon not available. We could not do investigation tests. We will do tests this morning, now he is stable." That word again.

"So there is stuff you can do for him? He will be OK? He's not going to die?"

"Yes," said Doctor Don, blinking, "there are things we can do. We are very worried about the arrhythmia. When his heart beats very fast, it does not work properly. His other organs are affected and it is very, very dangerous for him. We will try to find out what has caused this today."

"Can we see him?" asked Fraser.

"In a few minutes," said Doctor Don.

Nothing they could do for him that night. I exhaled, ran to the toilet and was violently sick.

I saw Andrew's feet before I saw his face. They were moving up and down, poking out from the end of the bed, visible from the door. He was conscious, alive. He still had the breathing tube, feeding tubes, wires and drips in every arm. I watched the heart rate monitor, the lit number fluctuating, edging towards one hundred and then back down again.

I stood beside the bed. He looked up at me and smiled slightly, although it was hard with the apparatus across his face. He lifted an arm, heavy with drips, and wrote in the air, motioning for paper and a pen. There was a clipboard on the side. I passed it to him carefully. His hand was weak and he struggled to write. He shakily drew a cup and a straw. He wrote the words "Orangina" and then "ice". I nodded. He underlined the words heavily. I nodded again. He held out his arm to take the pad again.

"Where I am?" he wrote, unable to put the words in order.

"You're in Bangkok," I started to write, and then remembered I could speak.

"You're in Bangkok," I said. I watched disbelief spread across his face. He furrowed his brow, squinted his eyes, and shrugged his shoulders as if he didn't understand.

"We took a jet from the Maldives," I said. "Your parents are here."

He shook his head from side to side. I held his hand.

"It's all OK. We are here now, and Rob's on his way. Even my dad and Iain are coming."

He looked surprised.

"Did I die?" he wrote.

I hesitated. If they had to shock him, did he die? "No, of course not," I said, "and you'll be fine now. It's all alright now."

He looked at me doubtfully, moved his head to the side.

"I think I died," he wrote.

He tried to move his hands to indicate that he hated the tubes, but he could hardly raise his other wrist from the bed. He made a laboured movement.

He started to write again and I tried to pre-empt his words; the writing was near illegible and muddled.

"You're thirsty? You're in pain? Are you in pain? Do you want the catheter out?"

He shook his head and wrote, "When I write not always bad."

I nodded and smiled. "I'm worried about you, is all," I said.

He was tired and sedated and his eyes began to drop. The pen relaxed in his hand. He jerked, half-awake again.

"I love you," he wrote.

"I love you too," I said.

His parents came into the room. Andrew stared at them, and a tear rolled down his cheek. His mum sat down beside him.

Fraser grasped Andrew's hand. "We love you so much," he said, like he would never see him again.

Chapter Fifteen

I heard my dad's voice before I saw him, familiar and reassuring. Tears filled my eyes and relief filled my chest. He looked hot and tired. He was wearing a short-sleeved work shirt, sensible trainers and a Sunbeam Alpine owner's baseball cap with a straight flat rim. My brother-in-law, Iain, stood beside him.

"I can't believe you're here," I cried. I was hardly able to make out my words. He wiped his eyes and hugged me tightly.

"It will be OK," he said.

I turned to Iain. "Thank you for coming. Thanks for bringing him here."

"It's absolutely fine. He would have been bloody useless trying to get here on his own. You know he gets a nosebleed leaving Chesham," he said, smiling. "Change in air pressure. We had to come. We had to be here."

He delved into his pocket and pulled out a small orange monkey. "George wanted Andrew to have this. It's his favourite toy, and he wants him to bring it home."

"Thank you," I said, crying properly now. Home felt so far away.

"He *will* bring the monkey home," he said. "He will," and then turned his head away.

I led my dad and Iain through to see Andrew. My dad hesitated at the door.

"Do you think we should go through? Do you think it's OK? We're not immediate family. Will that be alright?"

"It's fine," I said. "He'd like to see you."

Jenny and Fraser stood up and hugged Iain and my dad. Andrew tried to smile, but the tube in his throat made his mouth hard to move. To their credit, neither of them flinched. His parents and I had had time to get used to the tubes and the wires and Andrew looking so lifeless and thin.

"Thank you for coming for Lauren," Andrew wrote. "You OK?"

"It's no trouble at all," said Iain, "although everyone thinks we're a gay couple on holiday. I had to tell the hotel staff we didn't want a double bed."

Andrew smiled as best he could.

"How was the flight?" I asked.

"Brilliant, just brilliant," said my dad. "I really enjoyed it. I enjoyed it a lot, and we watched some good films, lots of good films. That *Ted* film, have you seen it? It's a little bit rude. The food was lovely, and I loved the view."

"He was shitting himself the whole way," said Iain.

"He looks OK," whispered my dad, once we were outside the room. "He looks much better than I thought he would. He's doing really well. He'll be absolutely fine now, no doubt about it, absolutely fine. He will be OK. He's a fighter, your Andrew. He's such a strong lad."

"He looks bloody awful," said Iain. "Let's be honest, but he's in the best place now. I just think it will take some time." He squeezed my hand and I felt better for knowing that they were there.

Visiting stopped between 2pm and 5pm to allow patients to rest, so we returned to the hotel. Nat took us to the lounge, where they served afternoon tea. Floor-to-ceiling windows looked out onto sunny Bangkok; the smog had lifted. There were low glass tables surrounded by gold embroidered chairs and matching sofas. There was a large counter at the far end, displaying plates and plates of bite-sized cakes: tiny cheesecakes topped with fruit, chocolate brownies and lime-green sponges, mini muffins, cookies in jars, rows of handmade chocolates, scones and jam. In addition to these were triangular sandwiches, smoked salmon, cream cheese, beef and onion, roasted vegetables, little chocolate mousses and pots of tea.

We huddled around a table. I couldn't eat. I couldn't speak.

They talked about Andrew, the hospital, the food. Fraser ate three scones, a round of sandwiches and a lime-green sponge. "He can still eat in a crisis," said Jenny.

"The food is delicious," said my dad encouragingly. "You should try and have a bit. I can get you a plate, or have some of mine." I shook my head.

A car came to take us back to the hospital at five o'clock.

I sat beside Andrew's bed. I stroked his hand and I stroked his head. I held the clipboard as he wrote the words "Orangina and ice" again and tried to draw glasses with bubbles and straws. The pen slid over the page, his hand was so weak.

"You can't have it yet. You have a breathing tube, but when it's out I'll get you them. I promise."

He shook his head and stabbed the pen into the paper, underlining the pictures.

"Not yet."

He tried to raise his hands in frustration but he didn't have the strength.

"OK, OK, I'll get it."

I walked alone to the small shopping mall opposite the hospital. The heat was thick. A traffic warden in a tall hat, white gloves and military-style suit, stood in the middle of a quiet road. He stopped imaginary traffic and beckoned me across. I nodded in thanks.

Christmas decorations hung from the ceiling, and piped Christmas music echoed through the walls. There was a florist on the ground floor directly by the door. The owner and her assistant wore Victorian-style dresses. The assistant had a hearing aid and I watched her boss sign to her. There was a Starbucks, a 7-Eleven, a bookshop and a deli. Taking an escalator to the second floor, there was a McDonalds, an Au Bon Pain cafe, a coffee shop, hairdressers and several restaurants. Nowhere sold Orangina. I cried hopelessly on the steps outside because I couldn't find the one thing he wanted, but he was fast asleep when I got back.

At ten o'clock, we returned to the hotel and sat silently in the bar. We made vague small talk and picked at a plate of chips. I retired to my room but still couldn't sleep. Half an hour later I heard a knock at the door and my heart jumped to my throat. Jenny Britton was standing there.

"Why don't you stay with us tonight?" she said. "Our bed is plenty big enough. I can't imagine you'll sleep on your own."

And so, ten days after our wedding, I found myself in the same bed as my parents-in-law. I slept for the first time in days.

Chapter Sixteen

Jenny B was a friend of a friend. She lived in Bangkok with her husband and two teenage children and had offered to do anything she could to help.

"Even if it's just doing some washing," she said.

I met her in the hotel reception before we left for the hospital on the second day, dragging my dirty washing behind me.

"Thank you. I am so grateful. I'm so sorry to put this on you. I just don't know where to find the laundrette in the city and they charge a fortune in the hotel, and I couldn't go through it. I couldn't look at Andrew's stuff. I feel so embarrassed for being so pathetic."

She was English, in her late thirties with dark curly hair and bright friendly eyes. She took the bags from my hand and hugged me.

"It's not a problem at all. I just wanted to help. We've lived in Thailand for a good few years now and I can help with anything you need – translation, medical advice, getting around. If you want a break from the hospital, you are welcome at ours. I guess you don't know how long you'll be here yet, but this is the least I can do."

I introduced her to the others as they walked wearily from the lift.

"I feel more anxious today," said Andrew's mum. "It's just the not knowing, it churns me up."

Faai was our translator for the day. She wore the smart hotel uniform, her lipstick was bright red and her long dark hair fell across her shoulders. She smiled widely as she approached us carrying several supermarket cakes and packets of biscuits awkwardly in her arms.

"For the nurses," she said, winking, "to treat Andrew the best."

"Did you cook them yourself?" asked Iain.

She laughed. "I don't cook! My husband does all the cooking, and all the housework. He loves to clean. My sister says he is more like a sister-in-law."

We arrived at the hospital and took the lift to the fourth floor. I felt nervous. My stomach lurched. I swallowed hard. I saw Andrew's mum do the same. She and I went through to see Andrew first. He was officially only allowed two visitors at any one time.

There was a group of doctors outside Andrew's room. We held back. They obscured the view. They spoke urgently, consulting the computer screens. They tapped their clipboards and directed the nurses. I could see his feet at the end of the bed, untucked, and they moved a little from side to side.

"We need to do emergency surgery now," said Doctor Don, blinking furiously. "We need to put a pump in his heart – heart not good." He demonstrated by making a fist opening and closing slowly.

"But you were happy that he was stable yesterday," said Jenny.

"His condition has deteriorated. He keeps having the arrhythmia and we need to stop this. You wait in the waiting room. It will take two hours."

I felt the brightness in the room burn behind my eyes and sickness in my stomach swell. Jenny took my arm as the room began to spin.

We stumbled to the waiting room by the surgical theatre. It was a small windowless room, with square oil paintings of single bright flowers magnified on the wall. There was a television showing images of the king on the news and a trolley of cups of water with pierceable lids and sharp thin straws piled beside. I stabbed a cup of water and it spilt all over the floor.

Fraser hunched over like an old man, wringing his hands, cursing the Wi-Fi as he tried to connect his phone.

"For God's sake, Fraser, it's not important," said Jenny.

He looked at her.

"I'm sorry, I'm sorry, Lauren. I don't know how you did this on your own," she said.

"I wasn't on my own. I had Tholal."

My dad held my hand. "He'll be fine. Of course he'll be fine. He'll be absolutely fine. There's nothing to worry about. It's the best heart hospital in the country, if not the world."

I nodded but couldn't meet his eyes. I wanted to believe him but I was terrified. Iain was silent, texting my sister, Jeanette.

I stared at the pictures on the wall until they blurred, and I wished and I prayed. "Please don't die, please don't die, please don't die."

Faai disappeared for a while. "I have been to the shrine," she said when she returned, "to pray for Mr Andrew."

"Am I allowed to go too?" I asked.

"Of course, I will take you."

I followed her through the hospital and out into the hot air. The shrine was the square marble area in the middle of the road I had seen when we first arrived at the hospital. The two huge elephants with stethoscopes stood guard on either side. Two large lanterns burned brightly in the daylight. A stone table faced an image of the god, covered with offerings. A metal pot of sand and ash glowed with joss sticks of different heights.

There was a smaller table behind, with pairs of elephants stood side by side. They were all different: plain, ornate, jewelled and painted, big and small.

"Why do people place elephants on the shrine?" I asked.

"Relatives put them there when a patient goes home, so the gods will watch over them and keep them safe. There are two: one for the patient and one for the family."

"And the drinks and eggs?"

"You can give a gift to the gods. Traditionally, people leave eggs, and the gods also like Fanta, but you can leave something that means something to you and Andrew. It doesn't have to be any of these things."

In the mall I chose a small row of Ferrero Rocher – and smiled as I thought of our first conversation – and a single orange rose, the same as my wedding bouquet, from the florists in the mall. The assistant wrapped it carefully in cellophane and tied an orange ribbon around the end.

We returned to the shrine. There was an old metal filing cabinet at the edge, with stiff, sticky drawers. Faai wrenched it open. Packets of joss sticks were stuffed inside, with every packet open, the sticks spilling out. She carefully counted nine and bunched them in her hand.

"Nine is lucky," she said.

She passed them to me. I set them alight from the lantern fire and shook them in the sunshine to suppress the flame. I placed the chocolates on the table. She motioned for me to kneel opposite the table and hold the lit sticks in one hand, the flower in the other.

"I've not done this before."

"You must say his full name," said Faai, "so the gods know who you pray for."

"I wish that Andrew Fraser Britton in room fourteen will make it safely through the operation and his heart will heal and he will get better. Please help Andrew Fraser Britton. Please help him, gods. Please save his life," I whispered just loud enough for the gods to hear.

I stuck my sticks between the others, still burning with the prayers of loved ones.

"I think of you all as my family," said Faai. "You are like my sister. I will pray also for Andrew every day until he is well again."

We returned to the waiting room, and waited again, until finally Doctor Don appeared at the door. "It has gone very well," he said. He didn't blink. "You may see him in a moment. The pump is working well."

Andrew was lying flat on the bed. If he sat up straight the pump wouldn't work. The surgeon had inserted a balloon attached to a tube connected to a large machine into his aorta through his groin. The balloon inflated and deflated using gas. The machine sat at the foot of his bed. It made a low harsh sound every other second and two honks like a wrong answer on a quiz show. He still had a breathing tube and wires in both arms. He reached for the pen and wrote, "I OK, relax."

"Because his heart not working well, very swollen, his other organs are not good," said Doctor Don. "His lungs have filled with water and his liver and kidneys are failing. We hope that the machine will improve heart function, reduce swelling and pump blood to these areas. We hope it will work."

I don't think I was capable of truly understanding how close Andrew was to death. I smiled and nodded and heard only, "It's gone very well."

Fraser and Jenny stood by his bed and watched him sleep.

I watched my dad and Iain exhale in relief. My dad's hands shook a little, and he steadied himself as he called my mum.

"She loves you," he said. "She wishes she could be here, but … but, you know."

"I know. She couldn't leave Jeanette and the baby on their own. It's OK."

He smiled gratefully. "You know she would have come. She would."

Chapter Seventeen

I spent that night with my in-laws in their king-sized bed, fearing that the hospital would call. I tried to sleep, fitfully waking in starts. I had frightening, vivid, lifelike dreams, every time I shut my eyes. I saw Andrew in front of me and heard the doctors speak. I saw tubes, machines, monitors and lights. I was terrified they weren't working. I woke in a panic, startled, screaming, sweating and shaking. Sometimes I stood up and tried to run to Andrew. I tried to pull drips from my own arms. I searched desperately for the wires. I gasped for breath. Where was my breathing tube? Where was Andrew? Where was I? I shouted into the darkness. Jenny grasped my hand.

"It's OK. It's alright. We're here. He's alright."

Rob and Karen landed in Bangkok the next morning. They came straight to the hotel and straight to our room. Fraser opened the door in his dressing gown. Jenny and I were still in bed. He hugged them tightly.

They looked exhausted. They had left home in their winter clothes, and their jeans and jumpers were creased and heavy in the heat. They stood closely together. Karen looked like she was holding Rob up.

"Don't tell me you all slept in the same bed?" said Rob, smiling weakly.

"They're plenty big enough," said Jenny.

"Ummm, bit weird," he said.

"How is he?" asked Karen.

"When can we see him?" asked Rob.

"We leave at half nine," said Fraser, "in a limousine."

Rob looked at his watch. "We'll see you in an hour then. Leave you to it."

They met us in the reception just before the car arrived. Karen was still steadying Rob. The eight of us travelled to the hospital in a minibus. My dad maintained a cheerful monologue, but no one answered. We were tired, and already the heat was heavy; it drained our energy. The worry sat high in my stomach and my hands still shook.

"It's two at a time," said Jenny. We had paused outside the intensive care ward.

"You go first," said Karen to Rob, "with Lauren."

Rob took a deep breath. I led him through the door and across the white marble floor to Andrew's room. Andrew still had a breathing tube; he still couldn't speak. He was thin and grey. He was watching the TV fixed to the wall. It took a moment to register that his brother was there. He stared, confused. His eyes filled with tears. He reached for the clipboard placed at his side and shakily wrote, "Thanks you."

"I wanted to be here," said Robert.

"Where is the prof?" Andrew wrote.

"She's here, she's here," said Robert, waving to Karen who was waiting outside, talking to the doctors and taking notes. "She's analysing the X-rays and asking about the medicines to speak to her friend on the cardiac team at Leicester hospital."

The corners of Andrew's mouth moved. He nodded.

My dad and Iain were in the waiting room. Faai was teaching my dad to text. Iain was reading a guidebook.

"I'm sorry there's so much hanging around," I said.

"It doesn't matter," said my dad. "We came to be here with you. We'll wait all day."

Iain nodded. "Don't start worrying about us as well."

The waiting room was busy with relatives. Some carried enormous cellophane-covered baskets of small jars of jam with brightly coloured bows. Some ate salty-smelling noodles from cardboard boxes for breakfast. I spoke with them a little. There was a young mother with her beautifully behaved seven-year-old daughter, whose husband was as sick as Andrew; Marianne, whose boss, Mama, was in the room next to Andrew and had travelled all the way from Qatar to receive the specialist help in Bangkok; and the Americans, whose friend was brain-damaged on life support after suffering a heart attack while holidaying in Phuket. They were all so saddened by our story. The other patients were far older than Andrew, but it didn't lessen their pain. I understood exactly how fearful the relatives felt.

"I'm certain they'll be fine. It's one of the best hospitals in the world. It's the king's hospital. They are highly experienced, and they'll be OK," I reassured them. I reassured myself.

I swapped in and out of the ward with Andrew's family, two at a time. We exchanged small titbits of information as we crossed. "His heart rate stayed stable. The oxygen levels look better. He's definitely got more colour."

"They'll remove Andrew's breathing tube if he can breathe unassisted for four hours," said Jenny.

For four hours Andrew breathed, and we sat by his side. We watched him inhale deep, careful breaths and exhale raspy, stilted air. We held his hand. I had never seen someone use so much concentration to do something taken for granted every second of every day. Eventually Doctor Don pulled the tube from his throat and we waited outside. Andrew screamed and swore in pain. I heard his first excruciating words in a week.

"Fucking hell!"

He beckoned me into the room and whispered in my ear, "Breathing is seriously underrated. Being able to breathe for myself is the best thing I've ever felt."

I nodded and held his hand. Tears of relief stung my eyes. I had missed his voice.

"Can I have that Orangina now?"

"I couldn't find one. I'm sorry, I searched everywhere."

His face fell.

"I am so sorry."

In the afternoon, Andrew was more awake. The balloon pump still beeped at the bottom of his bed, but he was able to sit slightly upright as long as he kept his legs straight. He was extremely weak but able to speak in short bursts. He was heavily sedated but I think he had some understanding of what was happening. Sometimes he spoke coherently. He told me to let his work know his situation. "I intend to be out of here by next week, but I'll probably need a week or so at home to rest before I return."

Luckily, both our employers had been hugely supportive and sympathetic and understood we would return as quickly as we could, but the situation was out of our hands.

A few moments later he would tell me to go to our allotment and pick the fruit.

"We haven't got an allotment."

"Yes, yes. I know that."

Rob and Karen walked around the hospital grounds while I sat with Andrew. They returned to his room with a brown paper bag.

"You'll never guess what we found in the cafe in the hospital," said Rob, triumphantly reaching inside and pulling out a small bottle of Orangina. He held a glass with ice and straw to Andrew lips and he took his first sip of fluid in a week.

It was a strangely euphoric moment. I felt absurdly emotional. Andrew's eyes lit up and he smiled broadly.

"Amazing," he whispered. "Thank you."

I was on a high from the Orangina. I believed him when he said we would be home soon. I believed that our life would just resume; we would return to work and in the future we'd tell stories of our nightmare honeymoon, safe and well.

Chapter Eighteen

The days that followed became reassuringly monotonous. I stopped sleeping in his parents' bed. I woke as the sun rose and stared at the city coming to life. I dressed and took the lift to the roof. I sat on a deckchair beside the empty pool and felt the early morning sun burn through the clouds. I turned the same pages of a book and tried to take in the words, and then leant over the edge of the building and watched the traffic swell below.

At 8:30, I walked to the breakfast room and pushed the tables together to seat seven. Rob arrived around the same time, after going to the gym and ordered an uninspiring cup of tea.

"What I wouldn't do for a Yorkshire teabag."

The others came and we shuffled around the buffet filling our plates. Markus, the manager, came to speak to us most days to offer support. I felt stronger and happier. I believed Andrew was on the mend. My appetite came back.

We spoke positively about the day ahead. Then we waited in the lobby for the car to arrive at 9:30 to take us to the hospital. Nat or Faai came with us to translate. We saw the same faces and the same things on the journey every day: the porter on the door with the too-short sleeves, the bald-headed driver who looked like a monk, the tyre man with his family, the familiar stray dogs, the traffic warden woman with the small white gloves, the uniformed man in the middle of the road with no cars to direct, the male nurse with the Cuban heels.

We took the lift to the fourth floor of the hospital, but for those few moments every day I felt overwhelmingly unsettled. I caught Jenny's eye. She had told me she felt the same. We waited in the waiting room until we were admitted through to see Andrew at ten. They were agonising, excruciating minutes, not knowing for certain if he was well, telling ourselves if he wasn't well the hospital would have let us know but desperately fearing the worst all the same. I looked for the families I recognised and breathed a sigh of relief when I saw them come out of the lift, still visiting.

Two of us would go through the doors into the ward and then one would return to the waiting room to tell the others the news. We worried if the update wasn't quick enough. We needed it immediately and then we could stop the sickening anxiousness churning in our stomachs.

For the first hour of each day, Rob and Karen looked at X-rays and computer screens and spoke with the doctors. Karen explained it to me clearly, but I don't think I really listened or understood. Andrew's condition was like a set of scales that the doctors needed to balance. The balloon pump was improving his heart function but there was water on his lungs. They gave him diuretics to drain the liquid, but they harmed his kidneys and he vomited violently. They prescribed drugs for his kidneys, but they affected his liver. They stopped the diuretics and his kidney function improved, but his lungs filled with water and so they started the cycle again.

Despite the setbacks, he seemed stronger every day, and I clung blindly to this.

I sat beside Andrew's bed. I held a cup of water to his mouth and helped him sip. I passed him urine bottles. I asked the nurses for ice and crushed it with a fork and fed him spoonfuls. I held cold compresses on his forehead and massaged his feet and his legs. I tried to feed him his breakfast in tiny pieces – spicy noodles or curries or tough overcooked meat – but he shook his head. I moved his pillows and adjusted his bed. When he was sick I held a bowl for him and wiped his mouth. I tried not to panic when the monitor alarms sounded, and I tried not to constantly watch his heart rate on the screen, fearing any incline.

His parents came to sit with him and I prayed for Andrew at 11am, alone on my knees at the elephant shrine, holding an orange flower and nine glowing joss sticks. "Please, no more arrhythmia.

Please let him be well enough to go home soon."

Rob, Karen and I ate lunch in the Au Bon Pain cafe in the mall at twelve. We sat in the same seats beside the same window and watched the same workmen on scaffolding welding the roof. They had no harnesses, no ropes, no protective clothing and no goggles. They wore thick black woollen balaclavas to shield them from the sparks in the stifling heat. They looked strangely sinister confidently lunging across the thin metal beams, the ground 30 feet below. They never fell.

Mostly we spoke about Monty, Karen's parents' dog. Rob ate unusual sandwiches: lychee and pistachio, Wasabi ham. "It's not unpleasant, Lauren, not unpleasant at all."

From 1pm until 2pm, I sat with Andrew, occasionally talking, when he was strong enough, and watching TV. I held his drinks to his mouth and tried to feed him thin soup. He waited patiently as the nurses took his temperature every half an hour, holding the thermometer to the light.

"No fever," they said happily, the only English words they spoke.

He held his arm out for blood pressure and gave his wrists for blood. He didn't scream when they stabbed him in the stomach with blood thinners, or burned the veins in his feet with potassium. He sat through the daily X-rays and ultrasounds peacefully detached. He was calm and I stayed calm too. I felt detached, like I was floating through the days on autopilot, but not hysterical.

A car came to the hospital to collect us at 2pm and we returned to the hotel. The seven of us sat in the lounge and ate more sandwiches and cakes.

We went back to the hospital at 5pm to sit with Andrew again. At 6pm I prayed at the shrine, and at 8pm we ate dinner in the mall.

At half past nine, I prepared Andrew's room for the night. I pulled the blinds, brushed his teeth, and put a cup by his lips to spit. I prepared the trolley by his bed and organised the items within easy reach: the sick bowl, the urine bottle, his water, a banana, a glass of ice. I made sure the call button and the television remote were close to hand. I adjusted the room temperature and put the side light on. I did all the things he couldn't do, or explain to the nurses how to do, once we had gone, and took in his face for one last time as he closed his eyes.

At ten, a car came and took us back to the hotel. His parents sat in the hotel bar. I stood in the shower. I couldn't cry anymore. My friends or my mum or sister called every night. They reassured me until I fell asleep, and then the day began again in exactly the same way.

Chapter Nineteen

We held it together as best we could. Jenny found comfort in facts and figures; she needed to know everything. She made notes in a blue bound book and looked up the terms and researched the statistics. She asked Andrew and the doctors endless questions.

"How do you feel? Does this hurt? Does that hurt?"

"How do you think I feel, Mum? Everything hurts."

She seemed calmer than Fraser in those first few days.

Fraser seemed on the verge of tears at all times, holding on to Andrew's hand like he might never see him again. He was visibly shaky and tense. He fixated on the positives, repeating any improvements over and over again.

He was desperate to do everything he could to help Andrew. "Shall I get you another blanket? Some water? An ice cream? Shall I change the TV channel? Do you want to sit up more?" He fiddled anxiously with his smartphone and smiled and smiled.

Rob and Karen were not unemotional but they were composed and collected. Unlike me, they didn't jump every time an alarm sounded, and they didn't question Andrew or try to help him until they were asked. They liaised with their medical colleagues in the UK and tried to retain normality as best they could. If they were nervous or frightened, I never knew.

My dad and Iain offered support and reassurance. They were patient and optimistic, but it was hard for them to watch me and not know what to say or do. They sat in the waiting room, hour after hour, day after day.

On the fifth day, Iain left. It was hard to see him go. He always made me smile.

"Make sure Andrew doesn't forget to bring George's monkey home," he said, and I hugged him tightly.

My dad left on the tenth day. I waited in the hotel reception with him for the car to arrive to take him to the airport and tried not to cry.

"We're so proud of you," he said. "You have been so strong."

"I couldn't have done it without you. Just knowing you were here helped me through."

He shook his head. "I will come back if you need me. I'll book another flight. It's not long, and it's not far. You just have to say."

I nodded and smiled and tried to hold it together.

"I love you," I shouted after him, as he dragged his suitcase to the door.

I met my friend Jeni's dad later that day in a coffee shop. He was travelling across Thailand with his wife. He gave me a huge soft toy monkey for Andrew from our pageboys and he cried when I told him Andrew was doing better."

"I only ever cry at happy things," he said.

I missed my dad and prayed he had landed safely, until he texted to say he was OK.

In the morning, a huge cardboard box arrived addressed from my friend Rach. It was filled with cards and presents from all my friends, heartfelt messages and words of support. There was chocolate, make-up, magazines and clothes, but most importantly, a box of Yorkshire tea. I slipped the tea bags into my pocket and made my way to breakfast.

Rob was sat at the table eating a bowl of thick fish porridge. "It's not unpleasant, Lauren. Not unpleasant."

"Nicer with a good cup of tea?" I asked, presenting him with the tea bags.

"It's a revelation," he said. "Thank God for Rach. I forgive her for giving my best man speech seven out of ten."

Karen left on 11th December. She took a taxi from the front of the hotel and Rob was quiet and withdrawn for the rest of the day.

On the twelfth day, the tests showed that Andrew's heart function had improved significantly enough to remove the balloon pump. The doctors asked Jenny and me to leave his room and they slid the thick glass door shut. Andrew screamed in agony as they pulled the tube from his groin. We heard him across the ward. It was louder than when they had removed the breathing apparatus. Doctor Don temporarily attached a clamp to the top of his leg to stem the bleeding. It was incredibly painful.

"Just five minutes," he said.

We returned to Andrew's room. Andrew twisted his head, ground his jaw, and clenched his fists. He squeezed his eyes shut.

"Tell me when it's time," he begged.

"Not long, you can do it, not long," his mum said.

I watched the seconds edge past. My eyes fixed on the clock. I stroked his head, but he turned away.

"Please let it be over. Please make the pain stop." He was white and wide-eyed.

After five minutes I called the doctor.

"Just another five," he said.

There were another five after that and another and another. He grasped Jenny's hand. There is nothing harder than watching the person you love in unbearable pain and not being able to help. No one spoke. I silently willed away the minutes and hoped and prayed for his pain to end. When finally the doctor removed the clamp, Andrew cried in relief.

"Thank God," he groaned. "I can get back to England and normality now."

I was so proud of him, and tears pricked in my eyes.

Chapter Twenty

The doctors moved Andrew onto the intermediate care ward, the ward for less-critical patients than intensive care. He had a bigger room, with a bathroom and an exercise bike. There was a large cream-cushioned sofa in the corner that turned into a bed and a couple of grey leather chairs at either end of the room. He still had heart rate monitors stuck to his chest, and oxygen, temperature and blood pressure observations every two hours. Drips still fed into his wrist and he was still catheterised, but he could sit up straight and swing his legs over the side of the bed and place his feet on the floor. It felt like huge progress.

The strict visiting times were relaxed, and Jenny, Fraser, Rob and I were all able to sit in the room with him all day. We no longer had to swap in and out of the waiting room. Andrew was no longer sedated, and he became increasingly frustrated with his situation and with everyone around him. The doctors had told that us once the water had left his lungs he should be well enough to fly home, but despite the diuretics, the water wouldn't shift. He wanted to walk, he wanted to stand, but he had no strength or muscle left in his legs. He wasn't used to being weak.

The medical staff obsessed about his urine output and restricted how much he drank. They asked hourly how much he had passed, and his parents and I did too. It infuriated him.

"I can't influence this. I drink my daily allowance of water which isn't enough to stop me feeling thirsty all the time, and all everyone does is go on about my urine. If I can't go, I can't go."

Rob stayed out of it. He kept a sensible distance, only involving himself when Andrew asked.

"Stop watching me. Rob, tell them to stop watching me. You can all go except Robert."

I was hurt, but I knew he wasn't himself. It wasn't a normal situation. He was strong and independent and suddenly he relied on everyone for everything.

Andrew hated the food and refused to eat. He pushed away the tray and snapped at anyone who dared to ask how it was. He hated the constant medical observations and the streams of doctors who came in and out of his room. He hated how we watched the monitors and jumped every time an alarm sounded. "It's just a drip needs changing. It's nothing. Just turn it off."

He was tired of the nurses not understanding him and the piles of pills he had to take each day. He was too weak to stand or to walk to the toilet, and he hated the indignity of the bed baths and commodes. He was still not able to do anything for himself. Even reaching for a glass of water was an effort, but he was reluctant to let us help him. We hovered around his bed trying to pre-empt what he might need, but it angered him further. He called his parents and me "The Spectres".

He withdrew into himself and hardly spoke. Even to his brother. He would not engage with us and watched the television intensely, film after film. He ignored my questions and pulled his hand away when I reached for him.

"What can I do to cheer you up? What can I get you?" I asked.

"Nothing," he said. "There's nothing anyone can do until this water goes from my lungs and then we can get out of this place."

"What about food?" asked Fraser. "What if I ask the hotel staff to cook you something? Would you eat that instead?"

Andrew shrugged his shoulders and turned back to the television.

Fraser spoke to Faai as we all sat at breakfast the following morning.

"Of course," she said, "anything we can do at all to help Mr Andrew. What would he like to eat? I will have it ready in half an hour."

"You look tired," I said.

"The Race of Champions is coming to Bangkok," she replied. "The racing drivers are staying at our hotel. We have a lot to do."

"What's the Race of Champions?" I asked.

"The Formula One racing drivers, and motorbikes. They make a race in Bangkok, people like Michael Schumacher."

Rob raised an eyebrow. He was playing *Cut the Rope* on his phone.

"Andrew loves Formula One," I said. "Do you think maybe that if we asked Markus the hotel manager, he might maybe be able to get Andrew an autograph?"

"That would be amazing," said Rob.

"I'll speak to Nat," said Faai.

"Operation Schumacher begins," I whispered to Rob.

"I see Markus in the gym every morning at 6am," he said. "You know he changes his shirt for every exercise he does. He's a machine. I've never seen him perspire, and he lifts really heavy weights and sprints for half an hour. Then he always speaks to me about Andrew, when I've just finished running and I'm dripping with sweat. I can hardly catch my breath and he wants to shake my hand."

"The man's a legend," I said. "There's nothing he can't do: free food, cars, accommodation, translators each day. No wonder he won manager of the year."

"Have you been stalking him on the internet?"

"No! They told me in the Maldives. His reputation precedes him. Why don't you ask Markus when you're sweating in the gym? Take another T-shirt like he does, and make a better impression."

"Why me?"

"He likes you best. He never shakes my hand."

"That's because on your first meeting you gave him an inappropriately awkward hug."

"Don't mention the weird hug. I'm still cringing."

"You know he dry-cleaned that suit immediately?"

"You weren't even there."

Markus was not in the gym the following day, but as we sat

drinking Yorkshire tea sneaked into a hotel hot water jug, he marched through the lounge, nodding at his staff.

"How is Andrew?" he asked, pausing at our table. I kicked Rob hard.

"He's doing well," I said, kicking Rob again.

"I would like to get Andrew something, perhaps some magazines," he said. "Is there anything he likes?"

"He loves Formula One," said Rob, "especially Schumacher. He loves fast cars and racing, motorbikes, that kind of stuff."

"Yes. Yes, I will get something like that," said Markus. "In fact, you know the Race of Champions is coming to Bangkok."

"Really?" we both asked (a little too innocently).

"He would love something related to that," said Rob.

"He would just love it," I said.

"I'll see what I can do," said Markus, smiling.

"He won't let us down," I whispered. "He's my hero."

We waited, and Fraser carefully carried a tuna baguette and chips in a foil-covered box to the hospital. He nervously presented it to Andrew, fearing his response. Andrew sat up straight and swung his legs to the side of the bed. He pulled a table in front of him and took a large bite.

"It's amazing, Dad. Thank you," he said.

He ate it all. I had not seen him eat properly in weeks. The mood in the room rose. It was a relief for all of us to have finally done something right.

"I'm sorry," he said. "I'm sorry I've been difficult and uncommunicative. It's just so hard. I hate being helpless. I've been horrible, and I don't mean it. A lot of it is down to hunger. I know I need to eat. I just couldn't stomach the hospital food, the noodles and rice. Already I feel stronger. Please can you do this every day?"

Fraser smiled. "Of course. Tell me what you want and I'll get it. We understand. We love you, and it doesn't matter how you've been."

That afternoon, a physiotherapist half his height helped him to stand for the first time. He was shaky and unsteady but his face beamed with joy. "Take a picture," he said. "I want to remember this moment."

I passed him the photograph captured on his phone.

"Do I really look like that?" he asked. He hadn't seen a mirror for nearly three weeks. I stared at the picture. He wore pale grey hospital pyjamas, too short in the leg and too short in the sleeves, but huge around the waist and hanging off his shoulder blades. His wrists were skinny and his feet swollen and scarred. His face was grey and his cheekbones pronounced. His eyes were sunken and wild, his hair long and colourless, matted and unwashed. But his smile was enormous. He looked so proud of himself.

"I look like a prisoner of war."

"It's not a great angle," I said. "You honestly look amazing. You should have seen yourself before."

"Come here and cuddle me," he said. He put his arms around me and I put my arms around him, like we always did in the morning before going to work or in the evenings if he'd been away for a night or if either of us felt sad or for no reason at all. I had been so terrified he would never hold me again. We stood for a few seconds. I felt every bone in his back. I gently pressed my head to his chest. I felt overwhelmed with pride at how far he'd come and how strong he was and how much I loved him.

"I love you," he whispered, "but I have to sit down."

Chapter Twenty-One

"Markus has something for Andrew," said Nat at breakfast. It was 18th December. "I'll let him know you are here."

Markus arrived moments later, dressed immaculately as always.

"I hope Andrew likes this," he said, pulling a poster from a tube. "It has all the signatures from the drivers from the Bangkok Race of Champions. They are all wishing Andrew well."

"I knew Markus would pull it out of the bag," I said to Robert.

Andrew was delighted. "It's the best thing I've ever had," he said. "Please thank Markus from the bottom of my dodgy heart."

He picked out all the names: Schumacher, Vettel, Coulthard and more I didn't recognise. He studied it for hours trying to decipher each signature.

Fraser had arranged for hotel food to be brought to the hospital daily, and Andrew was stronger and able to stand and walk a few paces along the ward. He could shuffle to the bathroom, and he asked me to wash his hair and help him shave. The doctors told us the diuretics were working well and the water was leaving his lungs. They drained seven litres in one day. Less pressure in his chest meant his breathing was less restricted and he was brighter and more positive. We were convinced he would be well enough to fly home for Christmas.

I was able to relax a little. I stopped panicking every day in the lift. I stopped obsessing about his heart rate and arrhythmia. I stopped worrying every time an alarm rang. Jenny seemed calmer. She asked fewer questions and Fraser stopped holding on to Andrew so tightly.

"You should have an afternoon off," Jenny said. "Fraser and I will stay here. Take a break from the hospital for a few hours."

"It doesn't seem right to sightsee."

"You don't have to sightsee. Just take some time for yourself, away from here. You're exhausted, and you need a change."

"My friend Paul, who you met on the first day, has invited us over for dinner with his wife and kids," said Rob, who was still playing *Cut the Rope* on his phone. "We could go for the evening."

"Please go," said Andrew. "I'm fine now."

Rob and I left the hospital that evening.

"Shall we take a motorbike taxi to the station?" I asked, as one skidded across the pavement in front of us and a nurse sitting side-saddle was flung from her seat.

"Let's take a cab," said Rob.

We negotiated a price and the driver agreed, but as we neared the station he started increasing the rate. He paused in traffic on an eight-lane road.

"One hundred," he said.

"You said fifty?" said Rob.

"One hundred," said the driver. I was scared he was going to lock the doors. Rob handed him a fifty dollar bill and swiftly opened the door.

"Come on," he said, pulling me into the road. We ran across eight lanes of traffic in the dark, dodging the cars. At the station we bought solid metal tokens and fed them into the underground barriers. We stood on the clear escalators to the platform and jumped on to the waiting train.

"It's five stops to Paul's," said Rob, settling into a seat.

I watched out of the window as we passed through Bangkok.

"There's the hospital," said Rob, pointing into the distance. "That's the stadium, that's ummm … some tall buildings, some houses."

"You should take up tour-guiding. You've got a real talent."

Paul picked us up from the station car park in his large four-by-four. His two-year-old daughter, Amy, slept beside me in the back. The streets were more suburban and less developed than central Bangkok. The buildings were lower, the pavements often missing, but the traffic was just as busy.

"It took me years to feel confident driving," said Paul, "and even now I don't understand how it works at times."

Paul lived in a gated development. There were rows of large white detached double-fronted houses. They were surrounded by low fences and grassless gardens. There were palm trees and large cars parked in the driveways. There was a swimming pool in the centre, a beautiful Japanese garden and a huge open lake surrounded by scrubland. Paul's house had a Christmas wreath hanging from the front door. Tiny pairs of shoes were piled in the porch, next to a red tractor and a child's pushchair.

Paul opened the door.

His youngest son, Eamon, shouted from the sofa, "They're here!"

The ground floor was open-plan, with white marble floors and a staircase in the middle. It was air-conditioned, cool and bright. A large television in the corner flashed with cartoons, and they had a huge Christmas tree.

Ryan, Paul's eldest son, was playing on his games console.

"Hi," he said, smiling casually. He was missing three front teeth.

"Come and see my trains!" shouted Eamon, grabbing Rob's hand.

"Give Rob a second, Eamon," said Paul, placing Amy on the floor. "Rob needs a drink first."

"I love my trains," said Eamon.

"Lauren loves trains," said Rob. "She'd be really happy to spend a few hours maintaining the track."

Eamon looked sceptically at me. He had met Rob before, and he knew he was good at smashing the trains into each other. He shook his head, still smiling.

"Come on then," said Rob, following Eamon up to his room. "Send a search party if I'm not down in an hour."

Paul's wife, Mon, was busy in the kitchen. She made me a drink, and I sat with Paul's mother, who had travelled to Thailand for Christmas. She was warm and friendly with a strong Irish accent. We spoke about Andrew, and I felt like I was telling someone else's story.

We ate a Thai curry around the dining table. I drank a glass of wine. At times I forgot the reason we were there. Paul told us how he had stood on a centipede in bare feet and it had bitten his toe. He said the pain was excruciating, and he was in agony for days. Mon took him to hospital but there was nothing they could prescribe. "I have never felt anything like it. It was the worst pain of my life."

The boys chased tiny cream geckos as we drank. They were almost the same colour as the floor, and I watched them dart up the wall.

"I love the geckos," said Robert. "I'd like one as a pet."

"I like pushing them outside with a broom," said Ryan.

"I like my trains," said Eamon with a mouthful of food.

"Why don't you both stay the night," said Paul.

"I haven't got a toothbrush," I said.

Paul's mum found a toothbrush from the plane in the depths of her luggage, and the boys showed me to the guest room.

"We watch cartoons in here at six o'clock in the morning," said Eamon, jumping on the double bed.

The air was heavy; a large fan in the corner of the room balanced on a chest of drawers whirred so violently it bumped up and down. My head spun with just the one glass of wine. I lay on the bed in the clothes I had come in. I watched the ceiling until the light began to fade. I heard Rob and Paul laughing downstairs.

I must have slept for a while as the house became silent. I was thirsty and hot and I went in search of a glass of water. I walked down the corridor past the boy's bedroom. The door was wide open where Rob and Eamon slept in twin children's beds. They both had their feet on the pillows. Eamon's head was halfway down the bed and Rob's was hanging off the end. Ben Ten bedspreads were tangled around their feet. It made me smile.

"I feel like shit," said Rob, trying to eat pancakes and bacon at breakfast.

"We were drinking until three," said Paul.

We walked carefully around the complex and the children rode on their bikes. I looked for killer centipedes, and Rob shouted, "There's one!" every few minutes, making me jump at the leaves by my feet.

We sat on the sofa and watched a film. It was nice to be normal, but slowly, unease crept up on me, until my stomach knotted and I felt physically sick. It had been less than half a day since I'd seen Andrew, but not being close to him made me feel unwell. Paul drove us back to the station and we returned to the hospital.

"Nice of you to see me," said Andrew.

"You said to go," I replied.

"Did I?" he said, shrugging. "Well, I hope you had a nice time, because I've been stuck with the spectre parents for days. There isn't anything I don't know about Dad's smartphone, and Mum keeps turning up the air conditioning 'cause she's hot from walking up the stairs while I'm freezing here and eating my food 'cause she doesn't want it to go to waste. They're driving me mad."

"It was just an evening." I felt tears fill my eyes.

"I'm sorry," he said, reaching for my hand. "I'm honestly pleased you had a break. I'm just so frustrated. I feel so uncontrollably angry sometimes. Thank goodness we'll be home in a few days for Christmas."

At 10pm we returned to the hotel. I was tired and I slept easily. Suddenly, a piercing sound filled the room. For a second I thought it was a smoke alarm, and then I realised it was my phone. "Andrew New" flashed on the screen. I answered, panicked, my heart thumping out of my chest.

"They had to shock me," he said quietly. "My heart rate went up to 200 beats per minute. They pulled my shirt open, put the paddles on my chest. I swear my whole body raised a foot in the air."

I tried to focus. "Are you OK, baby? It's alright. I promise. Do you feel OK?"

"I'm scared, really scared," he said. "I need you."

"I'm coming to the hospital now," I said, leaping from the bed. "It will take me ten minutes to get to you. You are going to be alright."

It was 4am.

I called Rob, my hand shaking as I dialled his room number.

"I'm coming. I'll see you in reception in two minutes," he said.

I ran to the reception and Rob was already there. He hailed a taxi outside the front. The driver drove swiftly through the streets, pulling in front of motorbikes, ignoring traffic lights and stop signs. There were no seatbelts and we were flung from side to side, sliding across the leather seats in the back. I was scared. It took less than ten minutes to get to the hospital. We dashed inside and jabbed anxiously at the lift call button and raced to the fourth floor.

The nurse in charge wouldn't let us into the intensive care ward.

"He is sleeping," she said.

"He called me. He needs us," I pleaded.

"You come back at visiting time."

"But he called. It's urgent. He had a heart attack."

"He is OK. He is sleeping, and you can see him at ten."

"Please, I beg you."

"I cannot let you in."

It was 4:15am. We looked at each other; there was nothing we could do. I tried to call his phone but it diverted to the answerphone. They had said he was OK. We pushed the large leather chairs together in the waiting room, made nests in the corner, and tried to sleep. Already light seeped in through the thin white blinds. I curled my legs under me and tried not to think of how he sounded, and the fear in his voice.

Rob called his parents and they arrived at ten. Doctor Don stood outside Andrew's room, studying a clipboard. "He had arrhythmia," he said, blinking. "His heart was very fast. It can be fatal, and we used paddles to shock him back to a normal beating."

"What caused this?" asked Rob.

"Low levels of potassium can cause arrhythmia. Diuretics reduce potassium and we have drained a lot of fluid from his lungs. We will have to reduce this. I think maybe it will take some time."

"But he is alright? He will be alright?" I asked.

"Stable," said Doctor Don, blinking frantically. "But it will take a few weeks longer."

We would not be home for Christmas.

Chapter Twenty-Two

The doctors adjusted Andrew's medication, and although he was stable, I felt unsettled and helpless. I started watching the heart rate monitors anxiously again. Jenny went back to asking hundreds of questions and Fraser got the scared look in his eyes. Andrew started suffering from panic attacks, waking terrified in the night and calling me, desperately begging me to come, but the nurses wouldn't let us in.

Rob began travelling to the hospital at 6am every day.

"I'm up anyway," he said. "Andrew will know I'm here if he needs me. He knows he's not alone."

It was three days to Christmas. Nat brought Andrew a small tree with tiny lights, but it didn't seem important anymore.

I had kept in regular contact with Jenny B, my friend who had washed my clothes in the beginning, and she invited me to her apartment in the break between visiting hours. We sat by the window and drank cups of tea. I recognised the hospital in the distance by the red heart sign on the roof.

Her family were preparing for Christmas. They had a huge tree towering over wrapped boxes below. The house smelt of pine needles, oranges, Sellotape and mulled wine. Her daughter and a friend were wrapping gifts in the living room, singing along to Slade on the stereo. Bags of presents were balanced on chairs, and Christmas pot plants and candles covered the large wooden table in the centre of the room.

Jenny had hand-sewn animals made from soft felt fabric to hide small gifts inside for her children. It was a tradition her father had started when she was young. The Christmas creatures were a closely guarded secret, hidden in the spare room, only to emerge on Christmas Eve. I loved the atmosphere. A perfect family Christmas unfolding, each ritual adhered to with effort and excitement.

"You won't believe it, but David and Robin have gone to get more provisions," she said, laughing, as they struggled through the door, armed with cardboard boxes of food.

Both her husband and son were tall and broad. They laughed about their Christmas shopping escapades. Robin was eighteen. His sister, Hattie, was two years younger.

"I asked the shop assistant where I would find the red cabbage. It's not a proper Christmas without red cabbage," said David, smiling. "And the girl says, 'No, we don't have red cabbage, definitely no red cabbage, never heard of red cabbage.' And then Robin points to one just behind her, and she looks at us like we're mad, and says, 'That's purple cabbage.'"

"The only thing we couldn't get was Brussels sprouts," said Robin in mock disappointment. "It's such a shame. I'm gutted."

"We like to have a proper English Christmas dinner," said Jenny, pulling chipolatas and vegetables from the bags, "even if it's forty degrees."

It was warm and welcoming in their apartment. It was the closest I had felt to home. I enjoyed their exchanges. I enjoyed helping them unpack. I missed my family.

"What will you do for Christmas?" Jenny asked.

"I don't think we'll do anything different," I said.

She looked at David and he nodded.

"Come here," she said, "all of you. We'll arrange it so it's ready in the break between visiting, same time as today. We can even make a little plate for Andrew. You don't have to stay very long. You don't have to do anything you don't want to do, but we would love for you to come."

"Thank you so much," I said, "but I will check with the others."

"Of course I'm keen," said Robert. "There are only so many Bangkok Plaza meals one man can stand, and the Christmas Paris ham and pistachio sandwich has nothing on a full roast dinner."

"Thank you. We'd love to," said Fraser.

Christmas Eve didn't feel like Christmas Eve. We didn't eat mince pies or drink mulled wine in the Rose and Crown surrounded by friends. It wasn't freezing cold, and I didn't still have piles of wrapping to do. I didn't feel festive but I didn't feel sad. The five of us sat in Andrew's room. We watched *The Muppets* movie and ate a McDonalds.

Andrew's heart rate stayed stable. It seemed to me the doctors had finally found the right balance of drugs. They gave him antidepressants and the panic attacks stopped. He was passing enough water without feeling nauseous. He was strong enough to stand for longer periods and walk across the room. He felt positive and we were too.

"The shocking was just a minor setback," he said.

I left him at half past nine in his intermediate care room.

"I'll see you tomorrow. I love you the most."

Chapter Twenty-Three

I bought red felt stockings for Fraser, Jenny, Rob and Andrew from a stand in the foyer of the hotel. I filled them with things I could find in the Bangkok Plaza: Au Bon Pain biscuits, sticky notepads, a line of Ferrero Rocher and a bottle of Orangina.

I left them outside their rooms and slipped notes under the doors. "Father Christmas says you have been 'not unpleasant this year.'" Jenny knocked on my door to thank me. She handed me a small bag. Inside was an "I heart Bangkok" T-shirt.

"I thought we could write heart hospital underneath," she said. "I have one for all of us, Andrew too."

The four of us ate breakfast in the upstairs lounge in our matching T-shirts. We looked like overly enthusiastic tourists. Nat and Julia wore Christmas hats. Christmas lounge music filled the room. They took a photograph of us standing beside the Christmas tree, smiling widely, arms around each other. Markus gave us each a voucher for a treatment at the spa.

We were in high spirits. We travelled to the hospital laden with gifts for Andrew: the stocking, the T-shirt, a huge basket of flowers, boxes of cakes and chocolates from the hotel. We walked through the ward to his room, chatting happily, wishing a merry Christmas to everyone we saw. They complimented our T-shirts and we smiled and said we hoped it would make Andrew laugh.

His room was empty. The door was wide open and the bed was without sheets. For a split second I thought he may be walking with the physiotherapist, but then I saw none of his things were in the room: the monkey, the Christmas tree, the pictures, the cards.

My hands started shaking, and my breath caught in my throat.

"It's probably something normal," said Rob. "They're probably cleaning his room."

"So where is he? Why haven't they called us? Why haven't let us know?"

"Andrew? Where is he?" Jenny cried at the nurses.

They looked at each other. They didn't understand. They couldn't speak English. They called the sister, who knew a few words.

"Intensive care," she said.

I dropped the presents and flowers on the floor. The room began to spin. I ran along the corridor, my heart racing and a painful pressure building in my head.

"Where is he? Is he OK?" I shouted.

Andrew was in his old room. He had an oxygen mask strapped to his pallid face. There were drips in both wrists and large machines and doctors surrounding his bed. He looked like he was sleeping, heavily sedated.

"He had a severe bout of arrhythmia early this morning," said Doctor Don, blinking furiously. "We shocked him. It is under control, but we are worried it may happen again. He must stay in intensive care, where we can watch him."

Suddenly I felt silly and conspicuous in my T-shirt. Fraser put his jacket on and buttoned it up. I walked to the toilet and cried over the sink. Andrew had come so far, and to be knocked back was devastating.

I rang Jenny B.

"I don't think we can come." I sobbed. I could hardly speak. "And we were so happy and so positive. I hate seeing him suffer. I hate this constant not knowing. I hate how things change every day, how you never feel calm, how you think things are going to be OK and then something else happens, and then something again. It's like every time we take a step forward, we take ten steps back."

"I can come to the hospital," she said, "if you need someone there."

"I'm OK. I'll be OK. It's Christmas Day."

"Please still come for dinner if you feel strong enough. We

would love for you to come."

I returned to Andrew and held his limp, lifeless hand. I told him all about our morning: the T-shirts, the presents, the staff in fancy dress. He didn't open his eyes. I tried to stop my tears from falling onto his face.

"I think we should still go," said Andrew's mum. "Visiting stops between two and five. What will we do otherwise? They won't let us stay."

"I want to be here for Andrew," said Fraser, "in case he wakes up."

"But Fraser, they won't let you see him," said Jenny. "You'll just sit in the waiting room and feel more miserable.

"You three go," he replied. "Bring me back a doggy bag."

Jenny B welcomed us in like long-lost family. The table was set beautifully with gold candles and flowers and seven place settings. The tree glowed in the corner and cards were strung from every wall. The smell of Christmas dinner filled the room. David bustled in and out of the kitchen with glasses of red wine. Hattie looked beautiful in a bright red dress. Robin crammed ceramic dishes of stuffing, potatoes, parsnips, cauliflower cheese and the famous purple cabbage between placemats and a huge shiny turkey.

"We are so happy to have you here," said Jenny, showing us to our seats.

"We don't normally dress identically at Christmas," said Rob.

"Just evenings and weekends," said David, smiling.

The food was delicious. We wore paper hats and drank the wine. I found myself laughing, despite everything. We spoke about Andrew, the wedding, Bangkok and the Christmas creatures.

David had made a creamed rice pudding with an almond hidden inside.

"It's really good," I said. "Lovely texture, great consistency, not too sweet."

"You've been watching too much *British Bake Off*," said Rob, laughing.

"Whoever finds the almond gets to make a wish," said David, and I searched through my bowl with my spoon.

"I've got it!" said Rob. "I think you know what I'll wish."

We left their apartment laden with Tupperware boxes of food. We were incredibly touched by their generosity and kindness.

Fraser was still sitting beside Andrew when we got back to hospital. "The doctors let me stay with him the whole day. I didn't have to sit in the waiting room. He's been asleep the whole time."

"Happy Christmas, Bubba," I said, kissing Andrew's head.

He opened his eyes a little.

"Is it Christmas?" he asked quietly, and then closed his eyes again.

Chapter Twenty-Four

A sense of sadness spread through us after Christmas. Andrew stayed in intensive care. He was barely able to talk. He was weak and drifted in and out of consciousness, unable to move. We went back to the waiting room, where the relatives we recognised were no longer there and we feared the worst. The journey up in the lift each day and the minutes until we could see Andrew were torturous. Progress was slow. We hardly spoke. Jenny and Fraser snapped at each other. I felt tearful and helpless. I read and read to stop myself thinking of anything else. Robert retreated into himself, spending long hours alone in the gym or walking. He seemed lost without Karen. He was distant and disinterested. He didn't smile or joke. It was like he was sleepwalking, following the routine: hotel, hospital, hospital, hotel.

"Ask her to book a flight," said Jenny. "She's still off work for Christmas. I think you need her. Fraser and I will pay if it's a question of money."

And so Karen came back, and almost immediately it was like a cloud had lifted. She didn't take over, but subtly things began to change. Information became clearer, the days seemed shorter. She listened and understood without asking what response I needed. Sometimes she gave me the truth and sometimes a nicer version of the truth. Andrew's condition improved and he was moved back to the intermediate care ward again.

She and I were sat beside Andrew's bed when a female doctor arrived.

"I think he has liver cancer," said the doctor without warning or introduction. "I need to check the figures fully and I will be back."

I looked to Karen and she shook her head sharply. I felt the familiar feeling of panic grow in my chest. "Please tell me the truth," I whispered.

"It's highly unlikely," said Karen. "He would have other indicators, huge amounts of weight loss, which admittedly he has, but that's also common with heart failure. He'd be a yellowish colour and he'd have a rash across his skin, particularly his face. I'll ask for those figures and send them to my boss. He's an expert on these things, and he will put our minds at rest. Honestly."

"Every time. Every single time. How can this happen? How can it be? Why Andrew? Why Andrew? He doesn't deserve this. Not cancer on top of everything else. It's not fair," I cried.

I was verging on hysteria and Karen led me from the room and into the hall.

"Please try and stay calm. There is a million-to-one chance that he has got cancer too."

"But there must have been a million-to-one chance he'd get heart failure on our honeymoon."

"I know, but we have to wait for the results, and as I said before, he doesn't have any other symptoms."

We returned to the room and there were doctors in white coats surrounding Andrew's bed. Fraser was hovering by the door; he was so tense he was unable to sit down. His eyes were red and he was clenching and unclenching his hands. Jenny was questioning the doctors with her blue bound book. Rob was listening calmly.

"What's going on?" I said.

"He's got a rash," said Fraser, "across his face and chest. They're the skin specialists."

Karen read my mind.

"It's just a coincidence," she said, still calmly. "It isn't what you think. Just because I said a rash and weight loss are indicators of liver cancer, it could be many things."

"They *are* worried," said Fraser. "It's come on so suddenly."

"We'll have to monitor his skin," said the doctor. "We will do more tests."

"What are these?" asked Rob, picking up a yellow plastic packet of wipes on the trolley beside Andrew.

"Lemony face wipes," said Jenny casually. "They cool him down, and he likes the smell."

"These aren't face wipes," said Rob, reading the packet. "'Antibacterial surface wipes. May cause irritation if in contact with skin' – when did you use these?"

"Oh, just before Lauren and Karen left," said Jenny, "but then the rash came on rather quickly after that."

"No shit," said Rob. "Let's try not using them and see if it goes away."

And sure enough it did.

When the doctor returned, Karen sent the cancer indicators to her boss and he responded within hours.

"The markers are indicative of someone with severe heart failure," said Karen. "There is absolutely nothing to suggest he has liver cancer; the possibility is miniscule. Interestingly, liver cancer is the most common form of cancer in Thailand, so they often check for this, but liver cancer is really uncommon in England. It is highly unlikely."

The doctor confirmed Karen's findings. The relief I felt was muted. I waited for the next knockback.

Chapter Twenty-Five

Karen, Rob and I were in Andrew's room on New Year's Eve. Jenny and Fraser had gone for a walk. Andrew was asleep. I was sat on the sofa half-watching a film I had seen before. A British Heart Foundation leaflet in English was on the top of Jenny's bag. "Inherited Dilated Cardiomyopathy" was the title. I began to flick through.

"There is no cure for cardiomyopathy," the leaflet read, "in most cases it can be managed by drugs."

I believed like any other muscle the heart would recover. I thought the drugs would reduce the swelling and he would have full heart function again. I thought he would be fine and our lives would return to normal.

"Most patients find they can continue with the activities they have always enjoyed, but at a slower pace. You may experience difficulties travelling abroad, getting a mortgage. Tests can be undertaken to discover if your children are likely to inherit the condition. In some circumstances, the condition deteriorates and patients may need a heart transplant."

The words began to blur on the page.

"Are you OK," said Karen, looking up from her book.

"Is this what he has then?" I asked. "It says he won't get better. He may need a heart transplant, and they advise caution when trying for children. This is all new to me."

Karen took a deep breath. "Yes, they think this is what he has. We thought you knew. We assumed you understood."

"I didn't. I don't," I said, tears running down my face. "I thought he'd get better. Everyone has said all along he'll be OK."

"And he will be OK. He'll just have to take drugs to manage his condition."

"But all the things he loves – the sport, the activity – it says *some* people return to work, *some* people are able to have children. What if he's not some people? This can't be happening. This can't be right."

"If you feel strong enough, have a look at the cardiomyopathy website," she said. "There's a lot of positive stuff on there. People live long, happy lives. They say they have met amazing people and made fantastic new friends."

"I don't need any new friends!" I shouted, and ran out of the room and outside the hospital. I felt foolish and stupid. I had buried my head in the sand.

Karen followed me. "You're not stupid," she said. "Your body was just finding a way to cope. Sometimes it's not the right time to process the information, and sometimes it takes a while to sink in. It's self-preservation. Could you have handled it before?

"I can't handle it now."

"You can and you will. You are doing amazingly well."

This was the point at which I started crying uncontrollably and couldn't stop.

"He doesn't know this. Andrew doesn't know this. We talked about having children and getting a dog and him going back to work. How can I tell him this won't ever happen?"

"It may still happen," she said. "Please don't write off the rest of your lives. Whatever life throws at you, you'll find a way through."

I followed her back to the ward.

"We thought we'd go into central Bangkok, watch the fireworks tonight," said Rob.

"I think we'll stay at the hotel," said Jenny.

"I'll probably go to bed," I said, trying not to cry. "It's just another day. It doesn't mean anything without Andrew."

"You should come," said Karen. "It won't be a late one. We'll count down to the New Year, watch the fireworks and come back to the hotel."

"Please go," said Andrew. "You can't spend it alone."

"You will," I said.

"I have nurses coming in every five minutes. I am never alone."

The roads were closed as the car edged back from the hospital at ten o'clock that night. The wide streets had begun to fill with people and stalls appeared at the sides of the roads selling coloured flashing Mickey Mouse ears, glow sticks and fizzy drinks. The crowds swelled steadily and families spilled from the stations, the hotels and the shops. Children ran excitedly in front of their parents, couples stayed close together clasping each other's hands, and large groups of teenagers in the flashing mouse ears shouted and screamed.

Rob, Karen and I changed and met outside the front of the hotel. Rob bought plastic cups of weak beer and vinegary wine from one of the stalls, and we joined the crowd edging towards the central area where huge screens had been erected either side of a stage. The minutes to midnight were projected on the tallest building and loud music blasted from speakers. "Gangnam Style" was playing on repeat. Everyone around us cheered as unfamiliar pop stars bounded across the stage and wailed into the microphones. The crowd screamed in excitement and thrashed glow sticks in the air.

"I love this song!" shouted Rob.

"You have no idea what it is! It's just noise and no tune."

"You sound like Fraser."

More and more people filled the space, squashing into us side by side. Large groups pushed past us to get to the front. Others just sat down and I stumbled into their bags. I was nudged in the ribs and poked in the back, and my feet were flattened by hordes of flip-flops, and weak beer and vinegary wine were split down my arms.

I felt entirely miserable.

"See," said Robert, "we're having an amazing time."

Last year Andrew and I had spent New Year in the Rose and Crown, with Darren and Caroline and Clive. We had drunk homemade raspberry vodka from an ice sculpture and picked at the buffet of sausage rolls and sandwiches. We had danced in the small space between the tables and the bar and wore silver paper hats and shouted at each other across the noise of the songs. At midnight, Andrew had kissed me as streamers and sequins fell at our feet.

I imagined he was probably sleeping by now. We should have been together. He should have been holding my hand. He should have been the first person I hugged, the first person I wished a Happy New Year.

The countdown began in English, the numbers flashing on the screens. My voice was lost within the tens of thousands.

"10, 9, 8, 7, 6, 5, 4, 3, 2, 1 – Happy New Year!"

Karen hugged me before she hugged Robert. "It *will* be a better year."

"I hope so," I shouted into her ear.

The fireworks exploded with a sound like cannons as the clock struck midnight. Each one was larger than the one before: fizzing, crackling, changing shape and made of vibrant colours I had never seen before. Huge domes and rainbows streaked across the sky. It was breathtaking and I wished Andrew could see them.

As the fireworks came to an end, the tens of thousands of people began to head home. Suddenly there was a mass of bodies behind me and in front, pressing and pushing, surging forward. My arms were clamped to my side and I couldn't move. People started shouting: some sounded panicked, some apologised for stepping on others, some calling out names. I shuffled to steady myself and I was shoved violently against a woman who looked at me in disdain. I felt feet under mine. I looked anxiously for Rob and Karen but they were lost in the crowd. I could hardly turn for people at my shoulder. I had strangers' legs and arms pressing into mine. I tried to stay as calm as I could. There was nothing I could do. "I'm really sorry," I repeated. And then, unexpectedly in front of me, I saw six-foot-high metal railings. There was nowhere to go but forward and the numbers grew. I was crushed closer to the people faltering at the front, scrambling to get over and smashing into the barrier. I had images of people trampled to death or impaled on the railings. I tried to contain the panic rising in my chest.

"Help me!" somebody cried, and suddenly strangers began to lift other strangers over the fence. I helped people to climb in front of me until it was my turn and I felt hands around my waist and fingers under my feet. I paused for a second to look back at the crowd. I saw Rob in the centre but I couldn't see Karen.

I fell into a large metal reindeer as I jumped down from the fence, and then I tripped over Santa's sleigh as I found my footing. The crowds had begun to disperse along the long wide road. There were still thousands of people but enough space to walk easily. I waited for Rob and caught my breath, desperately looking for Karen.

"We've lost Karen," I said.

"I saw her. She was in front of us. She'll head back to the hotel," he said, "Come on, follow me."

Discarded mouse ears lay in the street beside empty cans, wrappers, and the remainders of stalls. Everyone was still in high spirits, heading to the next party place.

Karen was in the hotel lobby when we squeezed through the door. Jenny and Fraser were sitting by the circular seating with thin glasses of champagne. They stood to hug me and wish me Happy New Year.

A Thai Michael Bublé impersonator sang, "I want to go home." I called him Thai-cle Bublé. Normally he made me smile, but as the adrenalin faded, I couldn't stop crying, tears sliding into my wine. I made my excuses and retreated to bed. I wanted to go home. Home with Andrew.

Chapter Twenty-Six

The first few days of 2013 passed without event. Andrew walked slowly but steadily up and down the long ward corridor twice a day. He had lost a lot of muscle and he was still incredibly thin, but colour had returned to his face and he was able to do most things for himself. Once again, we spoke confidently about finally going home. We waited anxiously for word of a date.

"I want to sleep in my own bed and walk to the pub and get back to work and not be monitored every hour," said Andrew. "I've had enough now."

I wondered if he knew the reality, but I never asked. I stayed positive in front of him and cried on my own every night until my head hurt. I willed my way through each day and never thought of the next until I woke in the morning and the routine started again: hotel, hospital, hospital, hotel.

The six of us sat in Andrew's room for hours on end. Sometimes Jenny and I walked to the end of the long dusty roads surrounding the hospital and peered into the huge gated gardens of the houses set back from the street. Outside it was hotter than ever, but we rarely saw the sun. Sometimes we sat in Au Bon Pain but mostly we watched television beside Andrew's bed.

"He has a blood clot in his heart," said Doctor Don on 5th January. "We need to give him medicine to make this go away. He will not be able to fly until the blood clot has gone."

"How long will this take?" asked Fraser.

"Eight to ten weeks," said Doctor Don, blinking.

We looked at him in horror. Eight to ten weeks.

"If that's how long it takes, that's how long it takes," said Jenny.

"We've got this far and we can keep going a little longer."

"I'll speak to the insurance company," said Fraser. "There must be something we can do."

I bought orange flowers from the florists and knelt at the shrine.

"Please let Andrew come home. Please let him be OK. Please let the blood clot go. Don't let it get worse or travel to his brain. Please let him recover enough to fly. I promise, I swear I will do anything. Please help him, gods. He's in room fourteen (there was no room thirteen). If you hear me, please let me know, please give me a sign."

At that exact same second as I finished, the floodlights surrounding the shrine burst into light.

"The lights always come on at six," said Rob.

"But I saw nine cream geckos sunbathing on the shrine, and they're your favourite and nine is lucky."

"Oh that's definitely a sign then," he said, shaking his head.

The following day a doctor from the insurance company came to see Andrew. His English was perfect. He looked at the charts and the X-rays and inspected Andrew's chest.

"I see no reason why the blood clot should preclude him from flying," he said. "He would be monitored by a doctor and a nurse constantly, all the way home. I think it would be better to get him back to England. I will make my recommendations."

And as quickly as that, plans came together to transfer Andrew home to England on 8th January. It was hardly enough time to gather my thoughts. I was happy to be going home, and happy that Andrew was well enough, but terrified about the journey. What if he didn't make it? What if the air pressure in the plane affected his heart? What if they didn't have all the equipment? At least he was safe here. I felt secure in our Bangkok bubble. I had not been home for seven weeks, and the thought of changing things filled me with fear.

Within a matter of days a plane to Frankfurt was scheduled to fly at midnight with Andrew and me on board. The insurance company used the term "repatriate" and I didn't like it. It made me think of fallen soldiers.

The plane was a scheduled flight with normal passengers on board. They had created a medical pod at the back of the jet, with equipment and monitors. Fraser looked it up on his smartphone and showed me the images.

"Andrew will probably go here," he said, pointing to the patient's bed.

We would then take a small plane from Frankfurt to Northolt RAF base, and an ambulance would transfer us on to Harefield Hospital.

Fraser researched specialist heart hospitals in England on his phone.

Harefield Heart Hospital was five minutes from our house. I remembered riding our bikes past the entrance and asking Andrew what they did, and him shaking his head. "I have no idea."

"Harefield Hospital is one of largest and most experienced heart hospitals in the world. A centre of excellence," read Fraser. "They carry out some of the most complicated surgery and offer some of the most sophisticated treatment anywhere in the world."

The insurance company could only arrange for me to accompany Andrew. Jenny, Fraser, Robert and Karen had flights provisionally booked for 15th January, but the airline would not change them. They begged and pleaded and explained the circumstance. They offered to pay a charge to rearrange, but the airline would not agree. They bought brand new flights via Vietnam leaving at midday, arriving three hours after Andrew and I landed. Twenty hours in the air and an airport stopover in Ho Chi Minh City. They used all their savings to take these flights. The thought of staying in Bangkok another week without Andrew was inconceivable.

Chapter Twenty-Seven

On the evening of 7th January 2013, AJ, our medical escort from the insurance company, arrived. He was an intensive care doctor in London employed out of hours to accompany seriously ill patients back to the UK.

"I've repatriated reporters caught in warzone crossfire, soldiers who've been shot, government officials and injured holiday makers. This is extremely straightforward for me," he said, smiling.

"I'll come and get you at 9pm tomorrow. Make sure you have all your bags packed. We'll take an ambulance to the airport, hop on the plane to Frankfurt, whizz across from Frankfurt to Northolt and before you know it you'll be back home."

He was fairly young, but his confidence put me entirely at ease. I stopped feeling afraid.

"We're going home, Bubba," said Andrew. "We're going home."

We ate breakfast for the final time in the hotel that morning. We gave gifts and cards to the hotel staff who had helped and supported us and we tried not to cry.

"Thank you for everything," I said to Markus. "You've been incredible. We would not have got through this without your support, the cars to the hospital, the food, the translation, the accommodation and all the little things."

He shook his head. "It was nothing," he said. "I am just happy that Andrew will be fine now."

I gave him an awkward hug and Rob sniggered.

The car arrived to take Jenny, Fraser, Rob and Karen to the airport. They hugged me tightly and I tried to keep composed.

"You can and you will do this," said Karen.

"We'll see you England, kid," said Fraser, and Jenny nodded and grasped my hand.

"Enjoy your final Au Bon Pain sandwich," said Rob.

I was on my own again.

I arrived at the hospital at the normal time. I gave presents to the nursing staff and doctors. I thanked Doctor Don profusely, and he didn't blink. I packed Andrew's bags, carefully. Jenny Beattie met me for lunch and then we waited and waited once again.

At just before six in the evening, I placed two small orange elephants onto the shrine beside the other pairs. I had bought them from a shop inside the hotel. The owner told me his brother had died from a heart attack. His eyes filled with tears when I said why I wanted them.

"Please take the elephants," he said. "It is a gift from me to you."

I asked the gods to watch over our elephants and watch over us and keep Andrew safe from harm. At exactly six o'clock, the lights didn't come on, and I wished Rob had been there to see.

The nurses gathered around Andrew's bed and asked me to take photographs. They smiled broadly and held up their fingers in a peace sign. They had learnt snippets of English.

"We will miss you, Mr Andrew," they said, and then giggled with their hands over their mouths and looked proudly at each other.

AJ arrived at nine. He held a small briefcase and a clipboard and he was not the slightest bit stressed.

"An ambulance will be here in a minute to take us to the airport. The journey should take twenty minutes. We'll be met by a German nurse from the flight at the entrance, who will guide us through boarding."

Andrew was wheeled outside on a stretcher and lifted into the ambulance. The nurses followed and waved excitedly. He shouted goodbye and smiled widely. I climbed into the front next to the driver and we headed from the hospital through the familiar streets of Bangkok until the skyscrapers faded into the distance.

A tall shaven-headed German man dressed in a smart red suit stood directly in front of the entrance to the airport departures. "I am the nurse who will be accompanying Andrew," he said. "He will be loaded on to the plane as cargo. You will need to check in as normal, please take your bags."

He handed me a ticket. "We will see you on the plane."

I spent an uncomfortable two hours waiting to board. I hovered by the gate. My stomach churned and my heart rate rose. I felt nervous and nauseous.

When my flight was announced I was upgraded to first class. I was seated at the front of the plane. My chair adjusted completely flat. They were serving champagne and cocktails on trays as I arrived.

"Where is Andrew Britton?" I asked, declining a drink. "The passenger in the medical pod? He is my husband. I'm worried."

"At the end of the plane," said the hostess.

I swerved through the passengers finding their seats, pushing past families stowing their bags.

The medical pod was where the toilets should have been, with the same grey plastic sliding doors. I knocked anxiously and AJ opened the door.

The room was tiny, windowless and dark. There was only a small space to stand, and my head skimmed the roof. Andrew was laid on a raised stretcher. The German nurse was seated at his head and AJ at his feet. Portable monitors flashed above the bed. Andrew wore an oxygen mask and there were drips in his arm. The nurse left the room and invited me to sit down. I stroked Andrew's head gently. He sat up so his head touched the ceiling.

"Welcome to the pod," he said. "It's cosy in here, although people keep thinking it's the toilet and getting the shock of their life."

"They upgraded me to first class," I said. "It's nice. I've never travelled first class before."

"And probably never again," said Andrew.

"So everything went well, getting on the plane, setting this all up?" I asked.

Andrew smiled wryly. "Ummm yeah, you could say that."

Immediately, I was worried. I looked to AJ.

"It'll all be fine," he said.

"What will be fine?"

"He's left my medication in Bangkok," said Andrew.

"You've done what? Are you messing with me?"

"I'm afraid not," said AJ. "In the confusion at the entrance about where to go, the ambulance team drove off with Andrew's pills in the back. I didn't have a chance to check I had everything until it was too late."

"But you have spares? You have alternatives?"

"Not exactly, but it'll be fine," said AJ.

"Just relax," said Andrew. "Enjoy your upgrade, enjoy the champagne. I'm getting my fluid through a drip."

"As if I can relax for the next thirteen hours knowing you don't have the correct drugs."

"Honestly, please, just chill out," Andrew said. "I'm going to try and sleep for most of the flight. You should do the same."

I zigzagged back to my seat past elbows and legs outstretched in the aisle. I pulled the blanket from the plastic pack and put on the socks. I adjusted the chair. I browsed through the films and I turned the pages of the in-flight magazine. I memorised the exits. How would they get Andrew out if we crashed into the sea? Would he make it? Would his bed float?

Every time the aircrew quickened their steps, I sat bolt upright, panicked, and waited for them to approach me. Every time I heard them talking in hushed tones, I felt bile rise in my throat and my shoulders tense. I prayed and prayed. I twisted my hair and bit my nails. I often forgot to breathe and took great gasping breaths as the aircrew walked right past me without a second glance. I was a nervous wreck. I tried to sleep, but woke fitfully every few minutes.

I couldn't eat the first class food and they took my tray away untouched. Every few hours I made the journey to the back of the plane to Andrew, but he became frustrated with my visits.

"Every time you open the door it wakes me up. Please, just let me rest."

It was a long thirteen hours.

In the same sky, Rob was crammed into a seat only big enough for a person half his height. His knees were wedged into the seat in front and his elbows were stuck tight to his chest. In another aisle, Jenny and Fraser, squeezed together, didn't speak. They didn't sleep. A single film showed on one tiny television, suspended from the ceiling just above Rob's head. He had to crane his neck backwards to catch the action, and the headphones hardly worked. They ate meat in a thick unidentifiable sauce. Their luggage was left in Thailand as it wouldn't fit on the plane. The aircraft jumped in turbulence and the overhead lockers shook. They had no idea if Andrew was OK and they wouldn't know for twenty hours.

Eventually, we landed in Frankfurt. The crew ushered all the passengers off from the front of the plane. I stood by my seat and let the queue pass until I could get to Andrew.

The plane was empty. There were papers and magazines piled on the floor and discarded cups and eye masks strewn across the seats. The aircrew bustled around us as we waited in the serving section. They helped Andrew into a wheelchair and put blankets around his shoulders.

"I'm not cold," he said.

"You will be," said AJ. "It's winter here."

He was right. When they opened the aircraft doors we were hit by the cold. Like a sharp slap. I was dressed in flip-flops, a light T-shirt and shorts. I hadn't thought it through. I sat close to Andrew and waited for instruction.

The crew began to unload the plane, and a raised platform to manoeuvre Andrew on to the runway was positioned by the door. AJ wheeled him on and I followed behind. A nurse from England smiled and introduced herself.

"It must have been so hard for you." She pushed a button and the platform lowered to the ground. It was dark and freezing cold.

To our left a tiny plane was waiting, smaller than the jet we had taken to Bangkok. The English pilot and co-pilot shook my hand politely.

"Should leave in the next ten minutes, depending on the

conditions. The flight will take approximately two hours," said the pilot.

Andrew was eased onto the plane a little like he had been before. Unlike before, the plane was functional – no flat-screen television or comfortable leather seats. It was old and basic and slightly damp. The windows were thick with condensation and it reminded me of the inside of a glider I had been in years ago. Andrew lay on a stretcher with the mobile medical equipment by his side. The nurse, AJ and I were crammed closely together. Our luggage was left in Frankfurt. There wasn't any space.

The nurse offered me a cold drink from a cool box by her feet. Then tea from a flask stuffed down the side of the chair. They adjusted the monitors until the plane was ready to take off. Andrew stayed quiet. He only said a few words. The nurse spoke gently to me. I don't remember what she said.

It was early morning and the sun had just started to rise. The red sky unfolded around us as we flew across the sea. The plane dipped and steadied just under the clouds. I pressed my nose to the cool window and wished us home safe. I tried to steady my thoughts. I tried to keep myself calm.

After about an hour and a half the monitors began to alarm. Andrew's heart rate had begun to increase. I saw the numbers on the monitor rise: 100, 103, 105, 110.

"I need a potassium infusion immediately," said AJ, stabbing a needle into Andrew's arm. The nurse found the bottle and calmly handed it to him.

"I have to stay calm. I have to stay calm," I told myself. "I can't distract them."

"Is he OK?" I asked.

"He'll be fine," said the nurse.

"How long till we land?" shouted AJ to the pilot, and then, "Can't we get there any quicker? Please can you try?"

The potassium steadied Andrew's heart rate. I watched the red figures on the monitor fall.

"I don't know how long this will last," said AJ.

"Will you have to shock him?" I asked.

"Possibly, we will do what we have to do."

I don't think my eyes left the monitor for the final half an hour.

Andrew stayed calm and breathed, and smiled weakly to reassure me. He reached to try and pat my hand. "I'm OK. I'll be OK. I'm not going to not make it so close to home."

"Five minutes to landing," said the pilot. I breathed a laboured sigh of relief as we touched down at RAF Northolt.

England.

We were finally home.

Part Three

Chapter Twenty-Eight

An ambulance was waiting on the runway. Two paramedics stepped down from the front and opened the back doors. They lowered a ramp so the stretcher could be pushed inside. It was a bitter English winter morning. The air was so cold it hurt to breathe. I was freezing and shivering. A thick fog curled across the landing strip.

I knew Andrew's family were still in the air. I desperately wanted to get a message to them.

I called my friend Katie. "Will you meet me at the hospital?"

I was terrified to be on my own.

"Of course, darling," she said. "I'll be there when you get there."

An official arrived and asked us for our passports. I passed them to him quickly as Andrew was being loaded into the ambulance. The nurse and AJ climbed into the back, and the ambulance crew shut the doors.

"Where shall I sit?" I asked the paramedic.

He looked at me blankly. "You can't go in the back, it's not allowed."

"What about the front?"

"There's only space for the two of us," he said, pointing to his colleague. "You'll have to find your own way there."

"It's the middle of nowhere. It's freezing. I have no coat, no car. I'm wearing shorts, and my closest friends are half an hour away. I have no English money for a taxi. I don't even know where I'd get a taxi from. I've travelled sixteen hours, not knowing if my husband would live or die, and you're telling me I've got to somehow make my own way to the hospital. Why can't I stay with him? There's space in the back."

The paramedic shook his head. "Policy."

"Let her in the back," said AJ. "I'll take the flack."

The paramedic raised his eyebrows and opened the door reluctantly.

The ambulance sped through the airport entrance, the sirens flashing. Andrew was quiet. "I am OK. Just tired," he said, his eyes rolling back into his head.

I was terrified. We struggled through the morning commuter traffic. I was surprised how many cars did not pull over to let the ambulance pass. We drove past the end of our street, past the chip shop, our doctors' surgery, the gym and the pub – everything looked so familiar but felt so unreal. In the early morning fog it seemed like a hazy dream.

AJ made insistent calls to the hospital. "Can you ensure you have this waiting? I need this, this and this." I couldn't understand what he was saying. I was scared. My teeth chattered with fear and cold.

We pulled up outside Harefield Hospital. A group of doctors in scrubs immediately gathered around the ambulance. They lowered Andrew from the back and pushed him up the slope and inside. I followed nervously behind.

Harefield hospital had been built during the First World War for the treatment of injured soldiers. It was an old-fashioned red-brick three-storey hospital, with long thin corridors and antique doors. The entrance building was H-shaped, and a small set of steps led to wooden double doors. There was a bright blue NHS sign above a window at the top and two thin windows at the side.

The interior was worn but welcoming. Scratched parquet tiles, ageing cream paintwork, chipped and marked walls. It reminded me of a Victorian school. It smelt of disinfectant and school dinners. The foyer was small and unassuming, and the windows let in little natural light, but the inside glowed luminously from strip lighting above. There were thin corridors to the left and right and ahead. Fundraising information was stuck to the walls above a row of comfortable chairs. Nurses and doctors hurried through, and porters pushed wheelchairs and stopped to chat to the receptionist who was almost hidden behind the high wooden desk.

It didn't feel clinical and cold. I liked it. Everyone smiled.

"Just stay here in the waiting area," said AJ, "until we know what's going on."

I sank into the seat and stared at the wall. Opposite was a mural made by local school children – paintings of hearts.

Katie was coming down the corridor before I had time to think. She was wearing a thick winter coat and thick winter boots. Her long dark hair fell across her shoulders and her cheeks were flushed with cold.

I jumped to my feet and started to sob.

"You're OK now," she said. "It will all be OK."

"Please don't cry," said the cleaner – he was pushing a broom across the floor – "This is the best hospital in the world."

I smiled, and thanked him, but I couldn't stop crying. Thick gulping tears engulfed me. Weeks of pain and fear and hysteria flooded down my face. Katie pulled me into her arms.

"I brought some things I thought you might need," she said. "Look at the state of you."

She fished out a jumper, leggings, a coat, water, food and magazines.

"You won't leave me? I can't be on my own again."

"I can stay all day."

"But what about your work?" I asked.

"Oh, I just walked out," she said.

AJ came to tell us that Andrew was stabilised. He and the nurse from the plane said goodbye.

"Thank you for getting him home safely," I said. "I can't thank you enough."

A Harefield nurse led me to room thirty-one. It was small and basic with a bed in the middle of the room. The equipment, unlike Bangkok, was not shiny and high-tech. There was no widescreen television. There was a large clumsy monitor to the left of the bed displaying Andrew's elevated heart rate. A side window looked out onto Portakabins and a small piece of grass. There was a blue plastic chair in the corner and a low wooden cupboard.

Andrew was propped up with pillows. He had a drip in his arm and an oxygen tube in his nose.

"Bubba, we made it," he said. "We made it home."

I hugged his skinny body, and my tears fell onto the sheets.

"It'll all be OK now," he said. "Thank you for standing by me and being so patient even when I was difficult."

That first early morning, the nurses bustled in and out. They were kind and attentive, efficient and calm. It was reassuring to understand what they said. I didn't have to mime everything, or translate every word.

Jenny, Fraser, Rob and Karen arrived at around half past two. I remember all four of them entering the room. I remember how they brought the cold in with them and how it surged through the door. They were wrapped up in winter clothes. I remember the look on their faces as they saw Andrew sitting upright. Absolute sheer relief. They clustered around the bed.

"The flight was appalling," said Fraser, "and they didn't put our bags on the plane."

I drank a paper cup of hot water in the canteen with Katie, Rob and Karen and pressed my legs against the radiator. My hands were numb from the cold. Jenny and Fraser stayed with Andrew; they would not leave his side. Rob and Karen returned home to Leicester when they were certain that everything was OK.

My parents arrived some time later that day and I met them in the entrance.

"We are so happy you're home," they said. "We felt so helpless so far away."

Visiting finished at 8pm and I suddenly felt disorientated without the Bangkok routine. The thought of returning to our home, suspended in time with its happy memories, filled me with fear. I didn't want to sleep in our bed without Andrew. I dreaded sitting on the sofa with an empty space beside me. I couldn't face cooking in the kitchen like we did together, me the kitchen porter, chopping and cutting, shouting, "Yes, chef." I couldn't face seeing his toiletries in the bathroom or his clothes on the floor. I felt entirely helpless and panicked to be on my own.

"We'll stay for a few days until he's home and well," said Jenny as if she had read my mind. "If that's alright with you?"

I opened the front door for the first time in seven weeks. There were wedding cards on every surface and unopened presents piled on the floor. An odd tiny silver piece of confetti wedged into the carpet caught the light. Our landlord had piled our post in the kitchen, but I turned away from the envelopes. Andrew's name on a letter made my stomach twist. I ignored the belated cards sent to both of us, "The new Mr and Mrs Britton." I went to our room and shut the door and cried.

I heard Jenny and Fraser sorting through our suitcases, putting our washing in the washing machine, boiling the kettle and cooking food they had found from my friends in the fridge. I should have helped them. I should have been a host. I should have made a bed up for them, made them a cup of tea and found them towels, but I couldn't move.

Jenny brought me a drink and some lasagne on a tray.

"I found his wedding ring," she said.

I held it in my hand and turned it over in my palm. I remembered us buying it together in York. He had taken me there for the weekend. We were excited about the wedding, excited to purchase the lasting symbol of our love, and now it wouldn't even stay on his finger, his hands were so thin.

"I'm sorry," I said. "Everything feels too much right now. I can't make sense of it. I want to believe he's going to be OK, now we're home, but I'm so scared. I'm still scared every second of every day. I can't keep doing this."

"We feel the same," she said, "but we have to stay strong. My good friend lost her daughter to cancer last year and she told me you just have to endure. It's all any of us can do. We have to look after each other, help each other through each day, and we will get through this."

Chapter Twenty-Nine

First thing the next morning, Jenny called the hospital. I found her hunched over the phone, carefully pressing the numbers. The nurses advised that Andrew'd had a good night, but we were not allowed to see him until 3pm. It was a long time to wait.

Fraser sat on the sofa and fiddled with his smartphone. He made exasperated calls to the airline, chasing their lost luggage.

"What do you mean it's in Bournemouth?"

Jenny and I went for a walk around the golf club behind our house and through the woods and down to the canal, a route Andrew and I did at the weekends. We hardly spoke. It was enough for me to just put one foot in front of another. All my thoughts were muddled and everything made me cry.

We ate more of the lasagne that my friends had left in the fridge and at 3pm we drove the five-minute drive to the hospital. Andrew was sitting up in bed drinking a cup of tea in room thirty-one, swiping his iPad. He looked good. He had fewer drips in his arms, and the heart rate monitor stayed stable at around eighty beats per minute.

"I feel fine," he said, "but I could do with a decent cup of tea."

We smiled, relieved. Jenny and Fraser got up to go to the canteen and my friend Rach came to sit with us. Suddenly the door flew open.

"Must be quick," said a tall white-haired man. "I am the most senior consultant here. I also run the hospital. Bottom line is: heart not good, will try an ICD first. Probably need an LVAD or transplant. Nurses will get you a leaflet. We *will* try to help you. We are in the business of mending hearts." He turned on his heel and closed the door behind him.

We looked at each other.

"He was nice," said Rach.

Andrew smiled reassuringly.

"There is no way I'll need a heart transplant. Look at me. I'm much better than I was in Bangkok. All I need is a few days' rest and I'll be fine."

Two nurses brought the leaflets as the consultant had promised. They explained that the plan for Andrew was to initially insert an ICD – an "Implantable Cardioverter Defibrillator" – essentially a pacemaker with three wires into the heart, which shocked Andrew if his heart went into an abnormal or fast rhythm, kept the pace steady and could help to remodel his heart, which was severely enlarged. If this did not work, an LVAD was a mechanical heart pump, a "Left Ventricular Assist Device". A pump was attached to the left side of the heart and a wire came out of the patient's waist attached to a battery pack. You couldn't have a shower or a bath because of the electrics and the risk of infection. "An LVAD is generally a bridge to transplant," the leaflet read. "Most people with an LVAD are able to lead fairly normal lives."

I passed Andrew the LVAD leaflet. He skimmed the first few pages and tossed it across the floor.

"There is no way on earth I'm having one of those," he said. "You can't even go swimming. Sod that."

"Have you read the leaflet already?" asked the nurse.

"No," said Andrew dismissively. "I'm not going to need one, so I'm not going to read it. It looks bloody awful. I'll read the ICD one."

"You really should read both," she replied, "and the transplant leaflet. You need to prepare yourself."

"I'll read it if and when I need to," said Andrew, hardly looking at them.

"Please just bear in mind it's an option," I said as the nurses left.

"The ICD will be fine," said Andrew.

"Everything OK?" asked Fraser, returning with a cup of tea.

"Absolutely fine," said Andrew.

In the days that followed, the staff at Harefield undertook many tests, angiograms and right-heart catheters to look at the heart, echocardiograms to measure the output, and chest X-rays and ultrasounds to see if the water had gone from his lungs. The doctors were incredibly proactive and they kept us updated, but because it was in English and we could ask more in-depth questions, everything seemed all the more scary and intimidating and real.

On the third day it snowed heavily. I trudged up the hill from our house to Harefield in wellington boots. Andrew looked out at the sheet of snow across the grass and watched the flakes settling from his bed.

"I would love to be out there," he said. "You know I haven't really been outside for over seven weeks."

"You will, Bubba," I said. "Once you've had the ICD in, you'll be able to go home."

"I don't want to run another marathon," he said softly. "I don't want to do a triathlon or walk Hadrian's Wall. I just want to feel well." The tears started to slide down his face. "I just want to be able to walk. If I can walk to the pub, I'll be happy. I'm not asking for much."

I climbed up beside him, onto the bed, and pulled his skinny body to me, stroked his face, and stroked his hair. It was the first time he had cried in front of me. He had been so brave.

"You will, baby, you will. I promise you will."

"I read the leaflet about transplants. Fifty per cent of transplant recipients don't make it to ten years. It's effectively a death sentence. Only ten years left to live."

"Statistics are rubbish," I said. "It won't apply to you. You are young, you are fit. It's probably people in their sixties who don't make it that long."

"But I'm not fit," he said sadly. "I can hardly walk to the toilet. I don't have the strength to stand. I can walk about three steps and I'm exhausted."

"You've been in bed for so long, it's understandable. You will be OK."

"Please don't go," he said.

Chapter Thirty

On 13th January, four days after we arrived in England, Andrew had the operation to insert the ICD.

"The doctor doing it actually helped design them," said Fraser, squinting at his phone. "He's the best ICD surgeon in the whole of Europe. He's had ten years' experience, and he really is the best."

My friend Victoria had had an ICD fitted the previous year. She'd had a cardiac arrest at a family barbeque, completely out of the blue. Her dad had acted quickly and given her mouth to mouth. He saved her life. She had stayed at Harefield for many months until she was well enough for the operation. Six months later, she returned to work and her life was fairly normal again. She was a real inspiration and extremely reassuring.

She talked me through the things I needed to do. Andrew's employer understood his recovery would take time and they were hugely supportive. I was able to take time off work, too, to stay with him. I was not capable of stringing a coherent sentence together, let alone function in an office.

The operation should have taken an hour. It was scheduled for 1pm. At 3pm, Jenny rang the hospital.

"He's still in surgery," said the nurse. "I'll call you when we know."

The waiting was torture. Jenny, Fraser and I sat in the living room.

"It's normal. He may not have gone down until later. He may be in a queue," said Fraser.

But as each minute passed slowly, the worry began to build.

"Is the phone plugged in?" asked Jenny, lifting the receiver and checking for a dial tone.

At 5pm we received word that he was out of surgery. We raced to the hospital. Andrew was in a bed on the main ward beside rows of men in their seventies. He looked pale and shaken. He wore an oxygen mask. He had a small scar, a thin incision, ten centimetres long, directly above his heart, like a top pocket.

The three of us sat beside him and pulled the curtains across on one side.

"I feel OK," he said, "but it was a struggle to get the wires in."

"It will take a while for you to feel any effects," said a registrar. "Some people find it can take up to six months, but you will begin to feel better. You just have to be patient."

"It's all going to be OK," said Andrew, and I genuinely believed him this time. He was exhausted and we left in silence at 8pm.

A man in his eighties was admitted to the ward urgently in the night. They laid him on the bed opposite Andrew and pulled the curtains across. Andrew watched doctors and nurses converge on the man's bed. He heard the man shout his wife's name and heard the nurses whisper comforting words. He heard a doctor call for a defibrillator and a nurse dash from the room. The alarms began to sound, screeching through the ward, and the shouts became urgent.

"Again, do it again." Then the high-pitched whine of the machine. "One more time."

Andrew heard the man die; he saw them wheel his body from the room.

"That was me in Malé," he said the next day. "That could have been me."

"But he was old," I said.

"It doesn't matter. I can't explain what it's like hearing someone die," he said, turning his face to the pillow. "I just need to be alone."

I left and sat in the cafe with my legs against the radiator. Leftover grey snow was scattered across the paths in clumps, and the building was filled with patients' friends and relatives huddled at metal tables like in a school canteen.

Already we had slipped into a new routine and the events of Bangkok and Malé didn't feel real. I told people what had happened, emotionless, like I was reciting a story that didn't belong to me. I had no connection with the characters, even myself. They would stare at me open-mouthed, saying, "I couldn't have got through that," and I'd shrug my shoulders and smile. "You do what you have to do."

Even Tholal seemed like a distant dream. I texted him to let him know we were home safely, and I sent him a present to thank him for his help. He called me sometimes on a crackly line and we shouted about the weather and how Andrew was. I saw my old life in flashes, but mostly being beside Andrew engulfed everything else.

We could not see him until three in the afternoon, and a steady stream of friends came to see me until then, to offer comfort and support. My sister and little George sat in the living room every other day and he tried to crawl across the floor, holding the monkey he had given Andrew tightly.

At 3pm every day, Jenny, Fraser and I went to the hospital and sat beside Andrew's bed. His best friend Nick came every other day, although he lived two hours away, bringing bottles of water and magazines and sweets. He was always upbeat and positive and calm, and it rubbed off Andrew.

"Nick's a good one," said Jenny. "So sensible."

"You should see him after three bottles of wine in Le Mans," said Andrew, smiling.

Andrew was still painfully thin, and his clothes hung off him like a "These used to be my jeans" weight-loss "after" photo. He walked slowly up and down the corridor outside the ward, carefully finding his footing, and lifted small weights. He ate all the meals hungrily, and we brought him crisps and chocolate bars and cups of tea in between. He was upbeat and positive and we never mentioned what would happen if the ICD didn't work.

We stayed until eight in the evening, when visiting ended. Sometimes I went out for dinner. I hated being in the house; without Andrew it didn't feel like home. Jenny cooked homely meals but I could hardly eat. I tried to watch television until I fell into bed. Mostly I felt numb. We all endured in the hope that Andrew would be discharged soon.

Chapter Thirty-One

The seventh of February was discharge day. A registrar came to see us. He looked at the charts and the figures. He pressed Andrew's tummy. He examined his neck. He looked at his ankles and observed the ICD top-pocket scar.

"You are responding really well to the drugs," he said. "You seem to have a propensity for retaining water, so keep a careful eye on your fluid intake and output. If you begin to get bloated, let us know straight away. But apart from that, everything seems really good. The water has gone from your lungs and your liver and kidney function has improved. Your heart output is better, and in my opinion you would need to seriously fall off a cliff in your recovery to need a heart transplant now. I'll complete the paperwork for you to leave the hospital around five this evening."

I looked at Andrew. I felt the tears sting in my eyes.

"Come here," he said, holding out his arms. He sat. I stood, my arms around his neck. We cried with happiness, our wet faces pressed against each other.

"We've done it," he said.

I called Jenny; they were in the supermarket. I told her what the registrar had said. I heard her voice become choked.

"That's amazing," she sobbed, calling for Fraser. It was the first time I had heard her cry during the whole ordeal.

Andrew left the hospital at six o'clock in the evening. He had three bags of medicine, thirty-five pills per day. Pills for blood pressure, blood thinning, heart function, beta blockers, diuretics, stomach settlers and potassium. He shuffled slowly along the corridor to the exit, pausing every few feet to rest against the wall and catch his breath.

It was dark outside. The air was freezing, biting cold. It stung my fingers and numbed my face. Fraser had parked the car at the bottom of the stone steps at the front of the hospital. Andrew clung to the railing and limped down. He was shivering violently, but he was determined. He could and he would do this.

I pictured his arrival home as a celebration. I imagined how happy he would be and how his face would shine as he walked through the front door. I had cleaned the house in a frenzy, fixating on things that weren't important, desperate for it to be perfect. I wanted him to notice and smile. I had filled the cupboards with his favourite foods. I thought he would be elated and excited, but he hardly spoke. He shuffled to the sitting room and stood against the radiator.

"I'm so cold," he said.

I made him a hot drink, but it was an effort for him to lift the cup to his mouth.

"I'm so weak and tired. I don't know what to do with myself."

Jenny offered him food. "I can make you anything you want." But he shook his head.

"Maybe just some cereal," he said.

I ran him a hot bath and he struggled up the stairs, clinging to the banister. I sat beside him as he sunk into the water. He was so thin.

"I know it will take time," he said.

"But it will be OK," I said. "You will be OK."

That night we slept beside each other in the bed, but his breathing was heavy and laboured. He made frightening gurgling sounds like he had done in Malé, and I watched him intently to check that his chest still rose.

"I can feel you staring at me. Stop it. I'm not going to die."

"I'm scared."

"You have no reason to be. The ICD will shock me if my heart rate goes fast, and you heard the doctor, there's nothing to worry about now."

I wasn't reassured and I couldn't sleep.

Chapter Thirty-Two

The days that followed were incredibly hard for us all. Jenny and Fraser had agreed to stay with us a little longer. I think deep down they recognised that things weren't right, but no one was willing to say it out loud.

Andrew was weaker and far more vulnerable than he had been in hospital. He could hardly stand and every movement took all his strength. He struggled to breathe and he struggled to speak. His stomach was bloated and distended by water already gathering again, but it was almost too much effort to swallow the diuretics, and the journey up the stairs to the bathroom was far too far.

He sipped small amounts of water, swallowed small spoonfuls of cereal and one or two crisps throughout the day. Jenny and I cooked him his favourite meals but he pushed them away, unable to eat. The energy that eating took left him exhausted.

He was frighteningly thin and his clothes hung off him even worse than before. He was freezing cold and he either stood pressed against the radiator or wrapped up in blankets with the heating on full blast.

"It will just take time," he repeated.

But as each day passed I saw no improvement. He became more tired and more frustrated.

He started staying in bed until midday, barely able to lift his head from the pillow. He needed to take his first set of pills at 8am, but when I brought them to his bedside, he told me to leave.

"But you need to take your pills."

"You can't control everything."

"I don't want to control everything, I just want you to take your pills at the right time."

"What, and you think if I take my pills at two minutes past eight, or I don't eat the whole of my sandwich or I eat an 'unhealthy' packet of crisps or I drink less than 1.5 litres that I'm going to suddenly drop down dead. You need to get a grip."

"But you don't take your pills just after eight. Sometimes it's not till midday, and you hardly eat anything, and the water is so important. You heard the doctors. You need to drink your water allowance to help your body heal. Why won't you help yourself?"

"I am absolutely fine. It will just take a while."

"But what about your bloated stomach? You know as well as I do it's a sign of things not working properly."

"I've just eaten too much."

"You've eaten nothing. Yesterday you ate two ice lollies and half a packet of Hula Hoops. You're not getting any nutrients or vitamins."

"Are you an expert on nutrition? What the hell do you know? You don't eat that healthily."

"I'm not sick."

"Neither am I!" he shouted.

The atmosphere was unbearably tense. Andrew could not get out of the front door except for his twice-weekly hospital check-ups. I was scared to be on my own, and Jenny and Fraser wanted to stay, but the house wasn't big enough. We tiptoed around Andrew and snapped at each other, unused to our habits. I worried and worried. I twisted my hair and hunched my shoulders. I bit the skin around my nails and rubbed my eyes until they became bloodshot. I tried to be upbeat. I ordered his favourite foods from his favourite restaurants – Chinese and curry – but he ate only a mouthful. I invited his friends round, and he put on a brave face but then collapsed in exhaustion as soon as they left. Jenny read everything she could about ICDs and cardiomyopathy. She downloaded leaflets and spoke to her doctor friends. Fraser immersed himself in the golf and the football, and all of us desperately tried not to say the wrong thing. It was impossible. Even when you thought you were doing the right thing, it was wrong in Andrew's eyes.

One morning he woke and his stomach was incredibly bloated.

"My stomach seems to be pressing on my lungs," he said. "It's making it hard to breathe."

"I think we should call the hospital," I said. "Just ask for their advice."

"It's probably nothing," he said. "I've probably slept funny. It'll probably feel better when I stand up. It's nothing to worry about."

"So why have you told me, if it's nothing."

"I won't tell you anything anymore then. I just mentioned one thing, and it's not a big deal."

"Shall we just ask the hospital anyway?"

"No," he said, turning away from me, pressing the pillow against his head.

I went downstairs and hovered by the phone. I asked Jenny what she thought.

"Just call and ask the question," she said. "It will put your mind at ease."

I found the phone number of the outreach nurse, carefully copied on the back of a card pinned to the noticeboard. I picked up the phone and dialled cautiously, and Jenny shut the living room door.

"That does not sound good at all," she said. "Can you bring him in, in the next half an hour? I'll arrange a bed for him, and I'll warn the registrar he's coming in."

I looked at Jenny. "They want him to come in. I can't tell him. He will literally go mental. He is going to be so angry I went behind his back."

We both went to his room. I explained what I had done.

"I told you not to call, but you know best, you always think you know what's best for me. I'm not going in, and they can't make me. I refuse."

"Please," I begged. "I'm sorry. It's only because I'm worried about you."

"My dad can take me in then, when I'm ready. I don't want you anywhere near me today."

I walked to the canal alone and sat on the stone steps and cried until my eyes stung and my head hurt. I felt so helpless and hopeless.

Jenny came to find me. "He doesn't mean it," she said, sitting beside me. "He feels like he's losing control and he's not himself."

"But it's so hard," I sobbed. "I've lost control too. I want to help, but there is nothing I can do."

"You have done nothing wrong," she reassured me. "You have to believe he recognises everything you've done. He just can't think straight, and he doesn't have the strength to say it or appreciate it at the moment. He loves you. He loves you so much. You're his rock. You're his everything. A weaker person would not have got through this, and you take this … this – for want of a better word – abuse and his unkind words, and you keep smiling and you keep supporting him and standing by his side, and when he's better he'll see this."

Andrew and Fraser returned from the hospital later that evening. The doctors had given him intravenous diuretics to reduce the fluid. He felt better and calmer.

"I'm sorry I was angry," he said. "I love you. I just want you to talk to me before you do things that directly affect me. It was only a little bit of water, and once I was in there they decided to give me the diuretics, but it wasn't a big deal. It wouldn't have mattered if I didn't go."

I had stopped blindly believing him by this point. I nodded, defeated.

"I have some concerns about your progress," said Andrew's consultant a few days later. She was friendly and sympathetic. We liked her.

She asked him to sit on the pink leather bed in the corner of the room. He removed his shirt and jumper and she inspected his chest. He sat upright and she tapped, with two fingers, the hollows of his back. She pressed his distended stomach and put the stethoscope to his heart. "I will make you an appointment to have a transplant assessment next week," she said. "I will also arrange for the water to be surgically drained from your stomach, as the diuretics don't seem to be working as effectively as I would have hoped."

"We were told the ICD could fix my heart," said Andrew. "We were told I would have to fall off a cliff in my recovery to need a transplant."

"Sometimes ICDs work well," she said carefully. "I am not saying you need a heart transplant. I just want you to be on the specialists' radar and have the tests to confirm. The majority of people wait many years for a heart transplant, so it wouldn't be immediate if that is the case. On the plus side, your liver and kidney function has improved."

"What did your consultant say?" asked Jenny when we got home.

"Really positive," said Andrew. "Liver and kidney function is good."

"She mentioned referring Andrew to the heart transplant specialist. She has some concerns," I said. "She's worried it would be risky to leave things as they are."

"It's merely a formality," said Andrew. "She did not say I need a heart transplant. Why are you always so negative?"

"I'm not negative. I'm just facing the facts."

"She did not say I need a heart transplant," he repeated. "She just said they wanted to do some tests. I am telling you this now and you need to believe me. I do not need a heart transplant. I know how I feel and I feel better every day, and if you can't believe me then I am not sure I can be with you. I need to be with someone who has got my back. You haven't got my back anymore. You are so negative all the time. You always think the worst."

I started crying. "How can you say I haven't got your back, after all I have done for you, after every single day? I love you with every bone in my body. All I want is for you to be OK. The reason I fear the worst is because the worst always happens. How can you not expect me to be frightened when something so unthinkable, so unbelievable, has happened to you and we never seem to get any good news? I love you more than anything. I'm just scared."

"I love you too," he said, "but please understand, I will not let this beat me. I will be OK. You just have to be patient. If I don't stay strong and stubborn, this thing will beat me. If I don't believe, if I don't have hope, if I just give up and roll over, I won't survive. Look at your friend. It took six months for her to recover, and they said she wouldn't make it. It's only a few weeks for me. I am going to ace that transplant assessment. If they want me to run for five minutes, I'll run for five minutes. I will not leave you. I will not die."

Chapter Thirty-Three

Andrew's consultant arranged for the fluid to be drained from his stomach and the transplant assessment to be completed on the same day. Andrew stumbled breathlessly into the hospital.

A nurse ushered us to Rowan Ward. We followed her along a long windowless corridor, through two double doors at the end onto another corridor painted a murky pale blue. We walked past rooms with thick wooden doors painted the same colour, with windows like portholes and old-fashioned brass doorknobs. The ward looked like it hadn't been updated since the 1940s. I imagined nurses in old-fashioned uniforms and small paper caps with war-wounded soldiers in thick metal beds. Inside, the rooms were modernised, and patients sat with their doors open, their televisions flickering.

There was a long painted mural on the corridor wall, trees and birds and flowers, designed to be cheerful. There were six priority rooms at the end, situated in a square around the central nursing station (a set of desks with computers and papers piled high). There was no natural light at all.

Andrew's room was large. There was a bed against the far wall, a flat-screen television, an en-suite bathroom, a set of drawers and a chair. There was a large window looking out onto Portakabins outside. There was a small mural of blue birds in the top corner of the room. There was a noticeboard pinned with transplant information.

"This is lovely," said Fraser, "and you've got a television."

Jenny had returned to Retford for a break. It was just the three of us that morning. The television only had one channel that worked:

161

BBC One. We watched *Bargain Hunt* and *Homes under the Hammer*.

We waited all day, until six o'clock when a surgeon came to insert the tubes into Andrew's stomach to drain the water. Fraser and I hovered anxiously in the relatives' area.

When we returned to the room there was a bag on the floor containing thick red-brown liquid attached by a tube to Andrew's back.

"It's strangely satisfying," said Andrew, "seeing it all go, feeling less pressure in my tummy. Will you take a picture and send it to Rob?"

"You're disgusting," I said, smiling.

They kept the drain in for the whole of the night. By the morning it had drained six litres, and the water still drained. Fraser and I returned at nine o'clock and watched BBC One with Andrew until he was due to take the transplant assessment at midday.

"I feel great," he said.

And Fraser and I smiled at each other in relief.

Suddenly the door to his room banged open and seven members of staff hastily gathered around the bed, led at the front by the transplant specialist consultant. We had not met him before.

"Is this normal that there are so many of you?" I asked. "Or is something very wrong?"

The consultant addressed Andrew directly. "We are concerned that you may become too sick to have a heart transplant, and once that has happened, it is very difficult to get you back to a position where you will be well enough. There is a small window of being sick enough to need a heart transplant and too sick to be able to have one. Your other organs are beginning to fail again because your heart is not working sufficiently, and they are not receiving enough blood, in particular your kidneys. If they deteriorate any further then it could be very bad news. Let me give you an analogy: imagine a normal plane flies at thirty thousand feet; your plane is flying at seven thousand feet and there are mountains at five thousand feet. I'll give you another analogy: imagine your house is right on the edge of a cliff and the side of the cliff is beginning to erode away and you are nearly falling off the end."

Andrew nodded carefully, respectfully. I thought, "We're not stupid, you could just tell it to us straight. I don't need cliffs and planes." My hands started to shake.

"We need to move you to intensive care and put you onto an intravenous drug called milrinone. This will be administered through a central line in your neck, so you will have to remain in hospital while this happens. This will increase your heart function and hopefully help to repair your kidneys and get you into a better position to have a heart transplant. We will then need to discuss you being put onto the urgent heart transplant waiting list." He turned and left as abruptly as he had come. Only an Irish nurse stayed behind, watching until they had left.

"I'll do the niceties now," she said. "I apologise for the ambush, and the shock of it all. I should first explain who everyone was. The man you spoke to is the lead consultant. He is the heart transplant specialist, an extremely clever and dedicated man with years of experience. He was with two of his lead cardiologists, a senior house officer, a trainee and the pharmacist. He likes to ensure everyone is in the loop to ensure you get the best possible treatment. It seems your condition has become more serious a lot more quickly than we first thought. Please, do you have any questions?"

Andrew shook his head. I looked to Fraser. He was standing by the window, surprisingly calm. My eyes filled with tears.

"I'm worried," I said.

"He is *the* absolute specialist in his field," she said confidently. "You are in really safe hands. The team in intensive care are brilliant, and they will look after you well. Please call me if you have any questions." She handed me her card. "Any time. I will arrange for the transplant team to speak to you about what that entails."

We looked at each other; Andrew reached for my hand from the bed, the drain still draining, and a drip in his arm. He rubbed my hand. "It will be OK," he said. "It will be OK.

The nurses came quickly to prepare to move Andrew to intensive care. They bustled around the bed, taking notes, checking his tablets, filling in forms. Fraser busied himself packing Andrew's few belongings into bags. He was surprisingly composed as he folded T-shirts and bunched-up socks.

"Don't call Mum yet," said Andrew. "I don't want to worry her. I don't want her driving in a state. Lauren, you call Rob and Karen. I would like them to be here."

I called Karen from the corridor. "I'm worried," I said, my voice breaking. "He wants you both here."

"We will be there. We'll leave now," she said. "I'll go and find Rob."

I returned to the room.

"I should probably call Jen," Fraser said. "It's not fair for her not to know."

"I want to get settled first," said Andrew turning to Fraser. "Dad, I want you to come with me, stay with me, when they wheel me along to the ward. Lauren, please call my mum."

The porters pushed his bed from the room, Fraser by his side. I stumbled behind. I saw him disappear through thick wooden doors, and I sat and waited in a room reserved for relatives. I wasn't hurt that he didn't want me to accompany him. It didn't register. I was relieved I didn't have to go through it alone. I was relieved to be directed and incredibly proud of how he had handled the situation.

Fraser returned a few minutes later. He sat opposite me and reached across for my hand. "It will be OK, kid. They said it will take half an hour or so to put the line in his neck and then we can see him."

I found it difficult to organise my thoughts. Yesterday he was due to have a transplant assessment and we hoped he would be too well to need a heart transplant, and now he could be too sick to have one and then what?

After half an hour, a tall male nurse with closely cropped hair, in bright blue scrubs, paused outside the door. "Andrew's family?" he asked.

"Yes," I said, standing, "how is he?"

"I'm Warren. I'm his nurse," he said extending his hand. "I'm sorry I didn't come and speak with you earlier, it has taken some time. But he's fine, all fine. He's told me about his car, his bike, and he wants a jacket potato for dinner. You can come through and see him."

Fraser and I walked through the double doors into the intensive care ward. We paused at the green hand sanitiser dispenser and carefully rubbed the liquid into our hands. The ITU ward was open-plan. The floors were white and the walls were white. There were fifteen beds in rows of three divided by bright blue paper curtains. Each one had a computer station at the end and a nurse in blue scrubs assigned to every patient, calmly adjusting the infusions and changing the lines. The patients were mostly sedated or sleeping, surrounded by monitors and drips. Some had thick tubes extending from their sides, attached to large clear tubs of thin red liquid. Some had huge dialysis machines whirring beside them. I remembered the beeping of a heart pump from Bangkok. It was organised and almost peaceful, despite the constant activity. The phone rang, the Tannoy buzzed, alarms sounded, beds were pushed in and out, relatives pulled up chairs and doctors and surgeons observed the screens.

Andrew was in the third line. He was one bed in from the end. The lady to his left had had a heart attack while giving birth. She was in a coma. She had not seen her child. Her husband whispered to her and stroked her hair. There was a photo of her baby on the wall.

Andrew was sitting upright. He had a large bunch of brightly coloured wires hanging from his neck. "I feel like a Christmas tree," he said, smiling. He was covered in an inflated sheet that made a low humming sound.

"What's that?" I asked.

"It's my huggy bear," he said. "It's amazing. Hot air is pumped into it, like an inflatable cover, but it's lightweight so it doesn't put any pressure on my chest. It's lovely and warm."

Warren dragged two chairs across and placed them beside the bed. Then he sat at the monitor and began inputting information.

"So the milrinone will stabilise Andrew," I said to Warren, "then presumably you can give him oral medicine and he can go home?"

Warren paused before he spoke.

"The milrinone is a very strong drug," he said. "It can only be administered intravenously. Andrew will stay in intensive care until the senior doctors decide what to do. There is a big meeting every Thursday. They may put him on the urgent heart transplant list. They may decide he needs an LVAD. I can't tell you. I'm sorry, but I will tell you as soon as I know anything."

Rob and Karen arrived and we swapped, two in, two out. I sat in the waiting room, shell-shocked. I was unable to process what we had been told. Jenny came a few hours later, her face panic-stricken and blotchy with tears.

"I hate being away from here," she said.

My friends and family came to comfort me but I felt hollow and lost.

Chapter Thirty-Four

Andrew and I had not spoken about the possibility of a transplant since the few days before. Now he held the leaflet tightly.

"I need to talk yous through this," said one of the transplant coordinators. He was Irish and softly spoken. He wore a white tunic with green edging.

"The tests have come back, and thankfully you are well enough to transplant. The milrinone has worked well and your other organ function has improved. We still don't have an enormous amount of time, and so we are going to put you on the urgent transplant list. This is because you are unable to leave the hospital and you wouldn't live without intensive medical assistance. A heart transplant is the best option for you."

"How long will we wait? How much time do we have?"

"We have time," he said calmly. "We do around twenty heart transplants a year. This year we have done nineteen already, which is a record."

"It doesn't sound very many," I said. "Why so few?"

"Even if the potential organ donor is registered as a donor, their family or their next of kin have the final say on if their loved one's organs can actually be donated. You have to bear in mind, even though these people have technically gone, they will look like they are just sleeping, and when these families have experienced such a terrible trauma it becomes very hard for them to make that decision, and the decision needs to be made fairly quickly. There isn't a lot of time."

We nodded. I remembered how I felt every time I had nearly lost Andrew, every time I thought I might not see him again and how I would feel about losing part of him after he had suffered so much. I swallowed back the tears.

"The donor heart is matched on blood group, size, antibodies and lots of other medical measures," he said. "If you are a larger person, you will need a larger heart. Normally we get the call to say there may be a match. We send a member of our team to check it out. If it seems OK, we notify you at this point. We then do around four hours' worth of checks on the heart to ensure it's pumping properly and working well. We never transplant a heart that isn't 100 per cent right. You will be prepared for surgery. You go to the theatre, and the surgeon will remove your heart and put the new one in. From then on it's just plumbing.

"The night of the operation you will be given your first dose of anti-rejection drugs. You will continue to take them for the rest of your life. Some of these drugs may have certain side effects."

"Like what?" I asked.

"Sensitivity to the sun, an increased risk of certain cancers, infertility, kidney problems," he listed.

Andrew reached for my hand and smiled.

"He said *may* have."

"I need to ask you to sign some paperwork," said the coordinator. "I need to ask you some questions. Would you be willing to take a heart from someone over sixty? A heart from someone who has had cancer, been a drug user? A smoker? I must emphasise that we would never give you a heart that didn't work properly, but many people die waiting for organs because they are not willing to consider these groups."

"Of course," said Andrew.

"What about the donor?" I asked. "Do we get to thank the family? Do we get to find out anything?"

"You can write to the family after around six months," said the transplant coordinator. "You pass the letter to me and I pass it to their transplant coordinator. You can include your address, and they can choose to get in touch with you if they want to."

"Any questions at all, I am always around. Anything you want to ask me, please page me or call me. I will get back to you straight away."

He left the ward. Neither of us spoke for a moment.

"How do you feel?"

"I feel strangely calm," he said. "I want to live. I want to live. I want to live and be with you. I know I didn't want a heart transplant, but there's no choice. I can't really think about anything more than that at the moment. I know that once I've had the operation, I'll wake up one day and look in the mirror and think I've got someone else's heart beating inside me, but right now I just want to live."

I took his hand. I couldn't begin to imagine how it would feel. The sadness of knowing that someone else had died. The sadness of knowing that another family had lost a loved one. The enormity of it was overwhelming.

"I need to focus on staying well enough for the operation," he said. "I need to make sure I'm eating and keeping strong."

I saw him move mentally into work mode, stubborn and strong.

The doctors moved Andrew into an intensive care side ward with only four beds. Most of the other patients were in recovery after open-heart surgery. The nurses joked that Andrew wasn't ill enough to be there. The milrinone was working well. The colour returned to his cheeks and he began to eat more and drink more. He rode on an exercise bike with the physiotherapists and walked across the room. He was insistent that his condition would not deteriorate, and he did everything he could.

The wait for a heart had begun.

Every day, Jenny, Fraser and I waited. We went to the waiting room at 11am. The official ITU waiting room was outside the ward. It had a glass roof and a window wall on the far side. There was two rows of chairs facing each other. Sometimes it wasn't enough when large families arrived, and they crowded in the corridor. There was a television without a remote and no one knew how to change the channel. There was a low bookcase and a coffee table filled with out-of-date magazines. There was an intercom by the door, and each day we pushed the buzzer and waited to be admitted, checking the clock on the wall and checking our watches and phones. "They've been over five minutes now and not answered, shall I ring the buzzer again?"

The families in the waiting rooms became our friends. We spent hour after hour with them in that one small room. We learnt the stories of their relatives in the ward: the lad who'd had a heart transplant after catching a virus, like Andrew; the young mother with the baby; the grandparents with valve replacements; fathers, brothers, sisters, wives and husbands. We rejoiced in their improvements and feared the worst when suddenly we didn't see them again. The third day, I didn't see the husband of the lady who had been beside Andrew. I prayed she had changed ward and I'd missed them. But I never found out.

Josh's story is not mine to tell. We met his family in the first few days: his sister, Lana, who was in her early twenties and pretty with short blonde hair, and his mum and dad, Lorraine and Darren. They were friendly and welcoming, always asking about Andrew, always upbeat and smiling and supportive. Darren was from London, with a strong accent, and Lorraine was softly spoken Scottish with curly brown hair. They made us laugh despite everything.

Josh had had a double-lung transplant eighteen months before. He had been born with cystic fibrosis. He had never been able to be active until he'd had the transplant and then suddenly he was at the gym every day. He had been well for eighteen months, and attended Lana's wedding. She showed me the photographs. Josh stood smiling in a smart brown suit in a line with the family, hugging his mum, laughing and dancing and spinning Lana across the floor. Six weeks later, his body had begun to reject the lungs. He couldn't walk. He couldn't breathe. He was attached to an ECMO (extracorporeal membrane oxygenation) machine that pumped air into his lungs. They were now waiting desperately for him to have a second transplant, but it was an uncommon operation. The new lungs needed to be completely perfect, and there wasn't much time.

The family stayed on site in the relatives' accommodation. They rarely went home. It reminded me of us in Bangkok, and I was grateful that we lived so close. Sometimes the nurses called

Lorraine in the middle of the night and she ran across the wet grass and the gravel to be by Josh's bed. In the morning her eyes were red with tears and shadows, but she never complained.

"We need the lungs to come quickly now," she said. "The machine he is on only has a limited amount of time it works for."

For three months, his three best friends came up every Friday night and stayed until Sunday evening. They spent their whole weekends with Lana, Darren and Lorraine in the waiting room or beside Josh's bed, watching films and football. They were Essex boys, loud and funny. They told us stories about the places they stayed at near the hospital, a bed and breakfast down a long unlit lane, with dusty cobwebbed rooms, creaky floors and frightening shadows where all three slept together, one on the bed and two on the floor, listening to each other snore.

"It's definitely haunted," they said.

I was amazed by their dedication and their commitment to their friend. They never, ever missed a weekend. Josh meant so much to them.

"It don't feel right being anywhere else. We want to be with him, helping him through," they said.

I drew comfort from knowing Josh was doing well. Each day he increased the time he exercised on a specially adapted bike that he could ride laying down. He was able to speak to his family a little and squeezed their hands. Lana brought her dog, Peggy Sue, to the hospital and we took her to the window outside Andrew's ward and pressed her wet nose to the glass. He smiled and waved awkwardly, his arms weighed down with drips.

"We'll get a dog when I'm home," he said.

We stood outside Josh's window and moved her paws to make it look like she was dancing. He smiled as best he could and tried to lift his arm to wave.

I worried that the time would run out for Josh. I prayed for him, almost as hard as I prayed for Andrew, alone in our bed, an Andrew-shaped hole beside me.

Chapter Thirty-Five

Waiting was hard. I kept my phone beside me. I hardly slept, fearing and hoping for the call that would save Andrew's life. I tried not to think about how unwell he really was. He looked better than before. He ate and he rested and he was positive and calm. Most of the time it was hard to believe that time was running out. Only occasionally did it hit me. I passed a Subaru – like Andrew's car – on the road, while driving to my friend Emily's house. He loved his car. I thought, "If he doesn't make it, I want Nick to have his car," and then cursed myself for even having the thought. I can't think that. He will make it. He will make it. He can't not make it. But it stuck in my head. I started to cry, and I was sobbing and shaking so hard I could hardly see the road.

"Oh, Lauren," said Emily, opening her door.

"I don't know what he wants. What if he doesn't make it? I don't even know if he wants to be buried or cremated. I don't know what music he would want, what words he'd want said. I can't ask him. I can't talk to him about it. I can't. I just can't. I don't want him to die."

"I don't want him to die either," she said, her voice breaking, "but if, God forbid, he doesn't make it, whatever you choose, it will be what he wants. You love him and he loves you, and whatever and however you do it, it will be the right thing."

We stood for some time in her kitchen. I tried to find my breath.

"You need some time out," she finally said. "You are at the hospital every day. Why don't you come to Jane's hen do tomorrow night? I know you said you were nervous and you didn't want to be away from Andrew, but you haven't had a night off in three months. It would probably do Andrew good too, knowing you are doing something for yourself."

I nodded. "I'll think about it."

The following day, Andrew seemed well. He walked a few paces and rode on the exercise bike. He encouraged me to go to the hen do, but I was reluctant.

"Your mum and dad won't be here though. They're heading home."

"It's fine. Rob's coming down for the evening. I'm not going to be on my own. He'll probably pick you up if you ask him nicely, so you can have a few drinks. It's important to me that you have a break. I'm OK. You heard the doctors. I'm perfectly fine."

"I know. It's just so hard when everything changes so quickly all the time."

"It's one night, Lauren. Relax. Have some fun with your friends."

I changed for the hen do in the bright neon lights of the hospital toilet and rubbed make-up onto my pale thin face. I looked tired.

I sat with Emily and Rach at one end of a long table. Rach bought me a glass of wine and then another and another. I felt my shoulders lower from beside my ears. I laughed with them and felt more like myself.

At 11pm Rob came to get me. The hens beckoned him in from the car park. He approached the table cautiously, smiling widely. "I'm not drunk enough for this."

The girls laughed about how much he sounded like Andrew, and made him say certain northern things.

"I'm still smarting about the seven out of ten for the best man's speech," he said to Rach.

"I stand by my score," she said, winking.

He stayed for a while and drank a pint of coke. Everyone wished Andrew the best. We drove back, and Karen's Arsenal mascot – Gunnersaurus – stuck to the dashboard, nodded over the bumps.

"How is Karen?" I asked.

"She's OK. Throwing herself into work. Like all of us, she's trying to stay positive, but realistic at the same time. You know you can call her if you want to talk?"

"I don't feel much like talking most of the time, especially not now when I can hardly string a sentence together."

My speech became slurred, and the small space inside the car became too small. I wound the windows all the way down and tried to take in the fresh air.

"Does it feel real to you?"

He shrugged his shoulders.

"Are you able to get out of the car unassisted? Or do I have to carry you?"

"Bugger off, I'm fine," I said stumbling to the door.

I burnt some toast and sat on the sofa, and Rob put on the television. Within seconds I was sleeping, my face stuffed into a cushion, my high-heeled shoes still strapped to my feet.

Suddenly a sharp ringing tone cut through the room. I still had my eyes shut. I heard Robert stand. I heard him speak in an urgent tone. "OK, I understand."

"What's happened?" I asked, pulling myself up straight, a dull ache spreading from my head. I felt dizzy and nauseous.

"It's the hospital," said Rob. "I need to go up to the hospital. The drugs are beginning to fail, and they need to put a heart pump in."

"Like Bangkok?" I asked.

"Yes, like Bangkok," said Rob, calmly picking up his car keys. "Stay here. It will all be OK. Just rest."

"I want to come."

"Please," he said, "Andrew doesn't want a fuss. He knows you've been out, and you're tired. He doesn't want us all there."

"What about your parents?" I shouted after him as he walked towards the door.

"I'll call them," he said. "We don't need them coming down yet. It will all be OK."

I stood to turn off the television and my knees nearly gave way. I couldn't think with the sound around me. My teeth started to chatter. I was shaking violently, and I felt sick and scared. I remembered Bangkok, sitting in the waiting room, praying for his life. I didn't know what to do. It was 2am. I rang Katie.

"I'm coming over," she said. "Don't you dare try to drive."

I couldn't stay in the house alone. I was confused and hysterical. I felt panic rise in my chest. We hadn't lived in our house long. We didn't know the neighbours well. The lady next door, Claire, had come to our door some weeks ago and asked if there was anything she could do to help. She had a six-year-old daughter and a new baby. I guessed she might be up.

I ran from our house across the wet grass and knocked on her door. My make-up was smudged across my cheeks and my dress was creased. I smelt of wine. She opened the door immediately, her face full of concern.

"Andrew has had to have a procedure. I don't know what to do, and it's serious, really serious."

"Get the car keys," she shouted to her husband.

"Rob is at the hospital. Andrew doesn't want me there," I cried. "I've done so much for him and he doesn't want me there."

She led me inside, hugged me tightly and made a cup of tea. I sat on the sofa and cried.

"I'm so worried. I'm terrified. I don't want him to die. I'm so sorry to bother you. I'm so sorry."

She and her husband listened and tried to calm me down. She asked me questions until Katie arrived about how Andrew and I had met.

Katie and I returned home and waited for Rob. I sobbed and sobbed, still drunk, hysterical and shaking, my head spinning. We fell asleep on the sofa. Rob came back at 5am.

"It's all OK. He's OK," he said. He looked exhausted. "The pump is working well; it's doing its job. But like in Bangkok he is now bedbound. They are stricter about him sitting up. He is much more restricted, but he is OK."

Jenny and Fraser arrived at 6am with their dogs in the boot of the car. They had left as soon as they had found out. They had grabbed what they could in the few minutes before leaving: a small overnight bag and things for the dogs. The spaniels tore through the house, bounded up the stairs, charged in and out of the rooms and jumped on the bed.

"I told them not to come," said Rob. "Especially not with the hounds."

"We had to come," said Jenny. "We had no time to put the dogs in kennels. They'll be alright. How could we have waited until the morning?"

"You're exhausted and no use to anyone at this hour," said Rob.

"I don't care," said Fraser. "We need to be near Andrew."

I knew what they meant. I tried to sleep but a hangover raged through my head. I bought Claire a large bunch of flowers in the morning and knocked on her door, sober, in the daylight.

"How is he?" she asked, and then, "You really didn't have to."

"You were so supportive," I replied. "He is OK,"

"Chloe has something for Andrew," she said, calling her little girl. Chloe came shyly to the door holding an envelope.

"It's a get-well-soon book," she said.

"She's put her lucky penny in the bottom," whispered Claire. "It means a lot to her."

At eleven o'clock we went to the hospital. I held Chloe's card in my hand. We waited in the waiting room and spoke to Darren, Lana and Lorraine about the night before.

"He'll be OK now. They act so quickly. We saw him early this morning. Not a great night. He looked well," said Darren. "He gave me a wave."

"How's Josh now?"

"Twelve minutes on the exercise bike." He smiled proudly. "It's the nights that are hard for him."

The Tannoy echoed across the room. "Josh's parents, Andrew's wife: you can come through now."

The door to the ward clicked, and we walked swiftly through.

Andrew was lying flat on the bed. The familiar heart pump machine honked at his feet. He looked grey and tired.

"Why did they have to do it so urgently last night? Is everything OK?" I asked.

"It's fine. It was pretty routine, to be honest. They just did it last night as the relevant doctor was available. It's nothing to worry about. Honestly."

I smiled and held his hand; it was swollen and puffy and purple in colour.

I believed him because that was what I needed to believe.

The surgeon came to speak with us as we sat quietly watching the ward. He was Italian, with a strong accent and small round glasses.

"We were very worried last night," he said. "Your condition deteriorated very quickly. I thought we may have had to put in an LVAD, but this is a good temporary solution. It seems to be working well so far."

"I don't need an LVAD," said Andrew. "I feel OK, just tired. If I have an LVAD, it means I'll come off the urgent heart transplant list and I'll have my chest cracked open twice. It's not happening."

"There may be no option," said the surgeon.

Andrew looked at me. "I'm not sure how much more of this I can take," he said. "I can't sit up. Have you ever tried eating lying down? I can't reach anything. I can't move, and imagine how difficult and complicated it is going to the toilet. All I can do is stare at the ceiling. I just need this to be over."

My eyes filled with tears. I stroked his head. "Baby, it won't be for long. This is only temporary. You are on the urgent list, and in the next few days some poor family somewhere will lose a loved one and they'll make the incredible decision for you to have their heart. It will happen. I promise."

He shook his head. "I know, I know. It's just the wait is so hard, and the guilt and the emotion and the pain and the indignity. It's so hard, Lauren. It's just so hard. I try and stay strong for myself, for you, for my parents, but I feel so weak."

"I've got a card for you from the little girl next door," I said. "Shall I open it for you? It's to cheer you up."

I carefully unsealed the envelope. There was a small folded paper book inside.

"Get well soon, Andrew," it read on the front. I passed it to him and he turned the pages. It was full of pictures she had drawn of things Andrew needed to get better: an ice cream, with "ice cream" written carefully underneath in capitals in different coloured letters; a bunch of flowers; some sweets and grapes. There was a drawing of Andrew and me holding hands, and then right at the back a traced orange penny with "My lucky penny" written underneath. The penny was inside the envelope.

Andrew's eyes filled with tears. He wiped them away with his swollen hand and looked through the book again.

"She's put so much effort into this," he said. "And to give me her lucky penny, it means everything."

I smiled, "It was really sweet of her."

"Sometimes things happen in your life, even tiny things that would seem insignificant to anyone else, but they make you feel like it's worth the fight. They give you strength to carry on," he said quietly.

He clutched the penny in his hand.

"This penny is so important to me. I want you to put a hole in it and get me a chain so I can wear it around my neck," he said. "I believe it will bring me luck."

I took the penny and put it in a separate pocket so I wouldn't mix it up with any other coins.

Chapter Thirty-Six

My friend Katie's birthday was on 7th March. Andrew had been lying flat with the heart pump for five long days. Jenny, Fraser and I spent every minute we could with him, swapping in and out of the waiting room, chatting to the nurses at the end of his bed. Jenny and I massaged his swollen legs until our fingers became sore. We brought him ice lollies and ice creams as they were the only things he could eat. Fraser downloaded films on his laptop and set up the screen so he could watch from his bed. He engaged positively with the nurses and was calm and brave. Our friends came after work and we followed the routine like robots: home, hospital, hospital, home. I tried to eat, and I tried to sleep, but I was physically and emotionally exhausted. Some days it was a challenge for me to dress or wash my hair. It was freezing outside and I didn't feel like walking or talking or watching TV. I just wanted to be beside Andrew and to know he was stable.

I had arranged to see Katie in the evening and her present was on the back seat of my car. My friend Corri was coming at lunchtime to break up the day.

The waiting room was busy already and there were relatives hovering around the Tannoy. We all watched the clock until eleven when the ward opened for visiting.

Darren pushed the buzzer. "Andrew and Josh's families, please," he said.

A minute later, the Tannoy sounded. "Josh's dad, you can come through, but Andrew's family, can you wait a few minutes? He's just having something done."

There was something in her voice that unnerved me. I leapt from my seat. "Can you be more specific? What does 'something done' mean?"

"He's just having his lines changed," the nurse said.

I sat back down and breathed again.

Fifteen minutes later, the Tannoy buzzed again to let us through. Jenny and I walked along the corridor and into the small ward. The blue curtains were pulled tightly around Andrew's bed. There was a flurry of movement. His nurse for the day was typing quickly into the computer.

"Can we go in?" I asked.

"Yes," she said.

Andrew was sitting bolt upright, despite the heart pump. There were doctors I didn't recognise hovering around his bed. Andrew looked panicked. His eyes were wide and confused and his face was extremely pale. He reached for me as I moved into the space.

"What's wrong, baby?" I asked.

"I need an LVAD," he said. "They are doing the operation in half an hour. I don't want an LVAD. I don't want my chest cracked open. I don't want that machine, and I'm scared, I'm really scared. I'm so scared." He began to cry.

Jenny was on the other side of the bed. She reached for his other hand. "It will be fine."

Later, the doctors told us that he had only hours to live. He was running on fumes. He had nothing left. If they didn't insert the LVAD, he would almost certainly die. We would be "making our arrangements".

The Italian surgeon came to see Andrew again, accompanied by the LVAD team. They stood around the bed. They explained the procedure and asked Andrew to sign a consent form. Andrew wiped his face and steadied himself. He asked sensible questions and nodded in agreement, like they were giving him the figures for next year's marketing budget.

"Ok, I understand. Can you can clarify that piece of information, please?"

"Obviously there is a risk," said the surgeon. "There is a one-in-five chance you will not make it through the surgery. It is ultimately your decision if you do not want the LVAD."

"I want to live," he said.

Andrew signed the paperwork and we sat, shakily, beside him. The LVAD team demonstrated the functions of the LVAD, attached to a flask of water. The electric motor made the water bubble.

"It's like a turbocharger," said Andrew.

The surgeon smiled. "Exactly," he said.

Jenny and I stayed with Andrew, and Fraser came through to the ward. We waited until they needed to prepare him for surgery. Andrew held my hand tightly. None of us really spoke. We didn't cry. We just sat straight-faced. There was no point in pretending.

"When I come out of surgery, the first thing I want to see is my penny on a chain," he said. "Oh, and an Orangina and ice, with a straw."

I smiled. "Of course. It'll give me something to do."

The operation would take around six hours. The surgeon took my phone number.

"I will call you when the procedure is finished," he said.

Jenny and Fraser and I watched as Andrew was wheeled towards the operating theatre.

"See you in a few hours," I called after him, holding myself together until he disappeared.

My friend Corri met me in the car park, and I ran through the hospital, tears streaming down my face, my hands shaking and my teeth chattering.

"What's wrong?" she asked, walking towards me.

"This can't be the last time I see him. This can't be it. He can't die. He was so scared, Corri. He was terrified. It broke my heart. He can't die. He can't die."

She hugged me tightly and walked with me back to the waiting room where my friends, Jeni, her husband Paul, and Amanda, had arrived.

"One in five is 80 per cent," said Paul. "Those odds are good, and statistics mean nothing. He is young, he's fit, he's not been sick before. You have to believe he will be OK. He will be OK."

"We need to get this penny sorted," said Amanda. "Let's find a key cutter's shop."

We drove to the local town, but nowhere was open or would put a hole in the coin. "It will break or crack the penny," said a few places. "We haven't got the right equipment to make a small enough hole."

We returned to Harefield. It was nearing five o'clock.

"We are not giving up!" said Amanda. "If I need to do it myself, I will."

The key cutter's shop was still open but the owner shook his head. "I'm sorry, but I can't do it," he said. "You could try Malcolm next door at the framer's. Say Paul sent you."

The framing shop was small. There were pictures and wooden frames leant against the walls and hung at all heights. Malcolm was busily hammering a mount. He looked up when we walked in.

"Could you put a hole in this?" I asked, passing the penny across to him. He held it in his hand. "It's kind of a matter of life and death," I said, smiling sadly.

"Of course," he said.

He took a drill and gently began to pierce the coin. The drill skidded from the coin and refused to pierce the copper.

"I'll try another one," he said.

He tried three other drills: different sizes, different drills. Each time it failed.

"I have to ask," he said, searching through his tool box, "why is it a matter of life and death?"

"My husband is having a huge operation at Harefield. It's his lucky penny, and he wants me to put it on a chain."

"This is important then," he said seriously, pulling out another tool. He gently hammered it into the coin, and finally, without splitting or cracking, the hole was made. "Phew," he said. "I was worried it wouldn't work. I don't need any money for this; just let me know he's OK."

"But you've spent half an hour," I said.

He shook his head.

"We need a chain now," said Jeni. "How about the place opposite?"

Across the road was the collectables store: a double-fronted shop, with antique desks, bookcases and old chairs on the pavement outside. Two windows were piled high with pictures, ornaments, vases and records. It was crowded with knick-knacks, some polished, some dusty. There were glass cabinets and cupboards to the ceiling, filling every space. A white-haired lady was sitting low behind the till, so I hardly saw her when I walked in.

"Are you about to close?" I asked; her assistant was bringing items inside.

"You have a few minutes," she said, smiling. "What are you looking for?"

"A chain to put this on," I said, reaching into my pocket. She held out her hand and I placed the coin on her palm.

She held the penny for a few seconds and closed her fingers around it.

"He will be OK," she said, without warning. "I feel him clearly. I feel his presence, and he is OK."

I looked at Jeni and Amanda, and they laughed nervously.

"He's having a big operation on his heart," I said.

"He can't move his legs," she said. I nodded. "He's stubborn isn't he? Always telling you what to do, never does what he's told. He's a strong character, and this will serve him well. He's going to be difficult once he's had this operation. He's not used to being weak. You tell him when he comes round, and he will come round, that Julie says he needs to do what he's told."

We laughed. "You're right, he's exactly like that."

"I have a chain for him," she said. "I have the perfect chain, but I won't have it until Saturday. Come back on Saturday. He'll be awake by then and I will give it to you."

"Thank you," I said. "Thank you so much."

"You love that stuff," said Amanda. "He has to be OK now. We need to tell him the story!"

We checked the time, and it had been six hours. I rang Jenny and Fraser. They were still sitting at home.

We went to the best pub in the world, the Old Orchard, set high on the hill looking out across the canals and lakes.

"You need to eat," said Jeni, and she ordered me some soup at the bar. As soon as she had sat down, my phone began to ring. Private number flashed on the screen. I knew it was the hospital.

"Hello," I said, my heart in my throat, my stomach contracting, the air only half-filling my lungs. My hands shook violently. I could hardly hold the phone.

"Lauren, it's the hospital. The operation went really well, better than expected. I am very pleased. When we put the LVAD in, the right side of the heart began to work, and Andrew is doing very well."

I thanked him, in a daze. Andrew was OK. I didn't cry in those first few minutes. I felt strangely numb. Jeni and Amanda hugged me tightly, tears rolling down their faces. I called Jenny and Fraser, and I heard the relief in their voices, but like me, with a little disbelief. I was not quite willing to accept it until I saw him alive and well, and we were not allowed to see him until the following morning.

The first twenty-four hours would be crucial. His body had gone through so much. Jenny and Fraser came to the pub, my parents and sister too. We raised a glass to Andrew, but we knew that this was by no means the end of the journey.

Chapter Thirty-Seven

I slept fitfully that night, fearing my phone would ring. I woke screaming, frightened I had missed a call, scared of the private number flashing on the screen. Jenny came into my room and climbed into my bed.

"I'll stay with you," she said. "You don't have to do this on your own."

She rang the ward first thing in the morning and a nurse confirmed that Andrew was stable and that he'd had a good night.

At 11am, as always, we were able to see him. He was in the same bed he had been in before. He was heavily sedated and his eyes were shut, but the colour had already returned to his cheeks. He had a thick breathing tube in his throat, oxygen wires in his nose and a food tube attached to a bag of yellow liquid. There were three monitors and a tower of infusions behind him, the thin tubes leading into his neck. I read the names: Viagra, furosemide, milrinone, heparin, adrenalin. The LVAD was beside the bed. A wire extended from the side of his stomach attached to a controller the size of a tub of margarine. A screen showed the output. It wasn't as frightening as I had imagined. One long wound from the bottom of his neck to just below his ribs was visible under his pyjama shirt, covered in white plastic an inch thick, like dry ski slope material. There were three large drain bottles set on the floor attached to thick tubes from his chest, and red liquid dripped slowly into them. The surgeons came in and checked the figures on the screen.

"I am happy," said the surgeon, smiling. "He is doing well."

We sat around his bed, talking to him loudly, hoping he could hear us.

On Saturday morning I went to the collectables shop before the visiting hours began.

"I'm pleased it's you," said the lady behind the counter. "I have the chain."

She placed a blue jewellery box on the counter and opened it. "I think this is just right."

I fed the penny through.

"It is. It's perfect, thank you. How much do I owe you?"

"Don't be ridiculous," she said. "Nothing. Just tell him what I told you."

"Thank you, that's so kind."

She shrugged her shoulders.

As I walked back to the hospital and through the reception, a nurse from intensive care stopped me.

"He's awake," she said. "We need to take the breathing tube out and then you can see him. We'll call you through."

Jenny, Fraser and I waited and waited for the call, and finally, when the Tannoy sounded, we jumped to our feet and rushed into the ward.

"You two go first," said Fraser.

Andrew was propped up with pillows. He still had the oxygen and feeding tubes from his nose and the groups of wires in his neck.

"Come closer," he said, whispering, his voice was hoarse, "close so I can see you."

I leant forward, so my face was almost touching his.

"Just remember, I love you," he said, and then turned to face his mum, "and I love you. Never forget that." His eyes closed and he fell back asleep.

When he woke again, I helped to put the penny around his neck and Jenny held an Orangina to his lips.

The next two days passed slowly, a routine of waiting in the waiting room and sitting beside Andrew's bed. We watched him sleep and spoke to him in short bursts. We offered him ice lollies and iced drinks from a small cool box we'd smuggled through the door.

Jenny, Fraser and I massaged his purple swollen legs for hours. I rubbed his bony back until my fingers hurt. He regained strength and was able to move to sit in the chair beside his bed with the help of two nurses. His voice returned, but sometimes the pain was too intense to talk. Sometimes he would struggle with a sentence and grasp for his morphine pen, press it to administer a shot of pain relief and then carry on. Sometimes he was too weak to fumble for the stick and his eyes glazed over. The intensive care nurse of the day bustled around his bed. They washed his hair, shaved his face with a proper razor and played chill-out music as they worked. "It's like a spa," said Andrew.

Andrew took photos on a Polaroid camera of all the nurses, printing their pictures and asking them to sign their names below.

Andrew was easy and undemanding. Every day the statistics improved. I slept more easily, reassured that it would all be OK now. The surgeon explained that the LVAD was a bridge to transplant. They would ideally look to transplant Andrew six months after the operation, when his body had healed, but he would go on the waiting list and wait for a match. I read the LVAD leaflet and studied the statistics. Small coloured stick men illustrated the outcomes of patients since 2010. Of a hundred, twenty were transplanted, twenty died, forty still had the LVAD in, and twenty patients had found that the LVAD had given the heart a chance to rest and heal itself – they'd had the LVAD removed and needed nothing else.

"Do you think it's possible he could be one of the ones whose heart just heals?" I asked Gemma from the LVAD team.

"You can't predict these things," she said.

"Imagine though. Imagine if Andrew was one of those. Imagine if finally something good happened to him."

She nodded. "You never know."

Chapter Thirty-Eight

It must have been mid-March when my phone began to ring at four o'clock in the morning. Andrew's name flashed across the screen. My first thought was that they'd had to defibrillate him again. I felt panic rise in my chest.

"Hi, baby," I said carefully.

"Where are you?" he asked.

"I'm at home."

"Where am I then?" he asked. I could hear the stress in his voice.

"You're in hospital."

"Am I in Ireland?"

"No baby, you're in hospital at Harefield. Remember, you had an operation."

"No," he said. "How can I have had an operation? Why am I in hospital? I don't remember anything. We were getting married and now I'm in hospital. What's happening to me?"

"It's OK," I said as calmly as I could. "It's honestly OK. You're alright. You're safe. I'll come and see you now. I'll call the hospital and check I can come in. I'm only five minutes away. I can be there in ten. Please don't panic. It's all OK."

"Please come. I'm really scared," he said.

"I'm calling the ward now. I'll be there in a bit. Try and stay calm."

I shouted to his parents, who were in the spare room. "I need to go to the hospital. Andrew's very confused."

I called the ward. The number was directly by my bed.

"I'm so sorry," said his nurse, in a strong Irish accent. "I didn't realise he was awake or had his phone. I could have calmed him down before he called you."

"He sounds very distressed," I said. "I want to see him. He wants to see me."

"He's gone straight back to sleep," she said. "Please don't worry. He's fine."

We waited until the morning. I couldn't sleep. I jumped at every sound, anxious he would call again, and worried he was scared. At eleven I pressed the buzzer and we were admitted onto the ward. The curtains were pulled around the bed. I pulled them apart and found him sobbing on the chair beside his bed.

"What's wrong? What's wrong?" I said, grabbing his hand.

"How can it be March?" he asked. "The last thing I knew it was November. We were going on honeymoon, and we had just got married."

"Remember," I said. "We went to the Maldives and you got sick. Do you remember? We went to the hospital and then you got really unwell and we flew to Bangkok and then back to Harefield. You were in Bangkok for six weeks and then Harefield for a month and then home for a month, and then back here and you have just had an operation."

He shook his head and then thought long and hard. "I think I remember a bit of the hospital in the Maldives, and then bits of Bangkok, I think. I remember a small Indian man shaving my balls," he said, smiling a little, "but I can't remember anything else. I don't remember going home."

"You came home," I said. "It was almost a month. Your friends came round, and all my friends. We got a Chinese takeaway and ate it in the living room. We came up to the hospital every other day."

"I don't remember," he said, panicked. "I don't remember at all, so why am I here?"

"You caught a virus, and it attacked your heart. You had to have an operation to have a machine put in to help your heart, and it's like a pump." I pointed to the machine by the side of his bed, the wire coming from his stomach. He looked distractedly at the wound running down his chest.

"OK," he said slowly. "So tell me again, why am I in hospital?"

"You had an operation," I repeated. His eyes opened wide, like the first time he had heard this.

"An operation? What kind of operation?"

"An operation on your heart, to install a pump to help it work better. The machine that controls the pump is by your bed."

I looked to Jenny who was sitting at the other side of the bed. She nodded. He reached for her hand and began to cry harder. "I don't remember anything," he said. "Why am I in hospital? What am I doing here?"

"You had an operation," said Jenny, calmly, "on your heart, to put a pump in."

He looked to both of us, confused, shaking his head.

"And it's March and I'm in hospital. I don't remember. I don't remember."

I showed him the Polaroids he had taken of the nurses. He pointed to Warren.

"That's Warren," he said. "I like Warren. I remember the names when I see the pictures. I just can't put it all together. Tell me again why I'm here."

I was terrified that he'd had a stroke. I sought out a doctor and tried desperately to explain.

"Andrew's really confused. He remembers little after November. There's a blank look in his eyes. Do you think he has some kind of brain damage? Is it possible he's had a stroke?"

The doctor shook his head.

"Intensive care can induce confusion: the morphine, the drugs, the lack of day and night, the sleep deprivation, the observations every hour, the alarms. It happens to many people. Please try not to worry."

But as always it was impossible not to worry. In the days that passed he recalled very little. I could tell he was pretending to remember so he didn't alarm us further, but when people came to see him, I saw the familiar blank look in his eyes.

"You remember so and so," I'd say about a volunteer who had seen him many times before the operation, or a doctor we had spoken to at length, and he'd nod half-heartedly.

"Yes, of course I do. I remember everything now."

But when he saw friends who had only visited weeks before, he greeted them too enthusiastically.

"It's so good to see you. I haven't seen you since the wedding."

He was completely coherent in everything else. It was just those few months he had lost. I think it was how his brain coped with the trauma. It was all too much to take in. I wished I could forget everything after the wedding.

Chapter Thirty-Nine

The memory loss just became another thing we accepted as part of his condition. Andrew grew in strength, and whether he remembered what had happened or not, it didn't really matter as he was making progress. Even now I don't think he fully remembers that time.

Every day he cycled on the exercise bike for ten minutes and marched on the spot with the physiotherapists. He was moved from intensive care back to the high-dependency ward, and we packed his few belongings into the grey plastic hospital bags.

Andrew's new room was on the other side of the square. He still had three chest drains set on the floor either side of his bed, but his scar was healing well. He still had drips in his wrists and lines in his neck, and the LVAD wire extended from the left side of his stomach to the machine that kept him alive, plugged into the mains.

The room smelt of school dinners, hours after the food trolley had left. It had heavy blue doors that wouldn't close quietly no matter how hard you tried. A disposable plastic apron dispenser was only half-attached to the door, so it rattled and clattered like a twenty pence piece in a washing machine as the nurses pulled out another one before they entered the room at least every half an hour. Repetitive alarms and bleeps added to the constant 24-hour noise.

Sleep deprived and in pain, understandably his mood began to darken. The nurses took his blood pressure and oxygen levels every two hours all through the day and night. In between, they woke him to change infusions and take blood. The catering staff visited at meal times and every few hours in between offering teas and coffees and replacing his water. The cleaners came, pushing mops across the floor, changing the bins two or three times, trying desperately to close the metal lids gently, but they made a clear clattering sound. The doctors came in the morning, prodding his stomach, feeling his feet, the physiotherapists at lunchtime, encouraging him to ride the exercise bike or walk across the room. Everyone was kind and friendly and understanding, but it was all too much. The nursing team were incredible, always offering support and a smile, not only to Andrew but to Jenny and Fraser and I. They knew the observations were intrusive and exhausting but they were bound by the procedures, put in place to keep the patients alive, and they worked around his requirements.

His parents and I bore the brunt of Andrew's frustration. He was uncooperative and unkind. He snapped at everything we did. We could do nothing right. If we were standing, we should be sitting. If we sat, we were in the way. We moved things he couldn't reach so they were closer and he was angry they had been moved. His room was the only place he had any control over. He felt helpless and angry.

The only time we saw the old Andrew was when Brian, the lead volunteer, a man in his sixties who had visited patients at Harefield for nineteen years, came to see him. He had a calm, kind, wholesome manner and a story to tell, and he never asked Andrew for anything.

Still, we came and stayed with him all day every day. We arrived at the hospital around 10am and stayed until 10pm. We pulled the curtains in the morning, we helped him out of bed, helped prepare his toothbrush and helped him brush his teeth. We helped prepare his breakfast and his lunch, brought him urine bottles from across the room, called the nurses when he was in pain, organised his drugs and helped administer them, filled his water bottles and helped him to drink, brought him ice lollies, rushing across the car park with them in freezer bags, crushing ice in a plastic bag at home with a rolling pin, desperately trying to keep it cool.

We brought in magazines and box sets to alleviate the boredom. We watched hours of *Game of Thrones*, the family trees set out in front of us to remember every name. We massaged his legs and arms and back until our fingers seized up. Jenny made Ragu. We plugged and unplugged electrical items and lugged in things that he had ordered on the internet from his bed: icemakers, fans, sound systems, gym equipment. They sat unused on the side. I prepared his room for night time, helped him brush his teeth. I arranged the items so he could reach them and organised his bed.

He was incredibly thin and malnourished, and the doctors advised that he needed to put on weight. They advised that the drains could be removed and Andrew could return home if the albumen levels increased in his blood. He began to eat fry-ups for breakfast, burgers at 10am, burgers for lunch and fish and chips for tea, with crisps and fizzy drinks in between. He wouldn't listen to me when I questioned what this would do to his liver.

"It's what the doctors said."

"But is it really what they said?"

I began to argue terribly with Andrew and his parents about food. I felt like the only sane person in the room.

"But he needs to put on calories," said Jenny.

"You can put on calories without eating junk food," I said. "What do you think endurance athletes eat? It doesn't have to be junk food."

"You wouldn't give a starving child in Africa fresh fruit and vegetables and nuts and seeds," she said.

"Neither would you give them burgers."

"You have to eat what you fancy when you're sick."

"Please leave it out," said Andrew angrily. "The doctors have prescribed fatty foods and so that's what I'm doing. Why do you have get involved?"

"I just want to help. I'm not sure I believe you."

"You are not a nutritionist."

"I've never said I am, but it's common sense. Eat rubbish food and you'll feel rubbish."

"You can't control everything."

"I'm not trying to control anything!" I shouted, storming from the room.

But maybe I was trying to regain some control. I had no control over anything. I missed Andrew. I missed our old life. I missed every single little thing I had always taken for granted. Not feeling sick every time the phone rang. Not spending every waking hour in the hospital. Sleeping easily, eating properly without worry filling my stomach where food should have been. Seeing my friends on a weekend and not on a ward. Working. The life we should have been living had been pulled out from under me and I could not control anything. I cried, angry, frustrated, helpless tears in the corner of the canteen and could not see an end.

I made the decision to stop asking anything. I stopped commenting or trying to help. I told myself I didn't care and I didn't need to know. If it was really important the nurses would tell me, and I had to stop fearing the worst. There was nothing I could do and I had to accept it, and the tension between us eventually eased.

After a month on Rowan Ward, Andrew's albumen levels finally increased. He was stronger and fitter and able to walk confidently up and down the corridor and ride the exercise bike. The doctors pulled out his drains in three sharp excruciating movements that caused him to howl in pain.

Gemma from the LVAD team came to train us all in how to use the heart pump. She showed us how to change the controller that controlled the volume and speed of the pump if it failed. She showed us how to change the batteries, which lasted approximately two hours. She told us what to do in an emergency and what to look out for. The wire from his stomach was an open wound that could not heal over. She showed me how to remove the complicated dressing carefully, in a wholly sterile environment. She showed me how to set up a sterile space, how to put medical gloves on without any contamination, how to check for infection, clean the wound thoroughly and reapply the dressing – a series of thick plasters, gauze, clear tape and a plastic tax disc to hold it in place. The LVAD was a huge responsibility. Andrew could not leave the house without spare batteries and a spare controller. He would die within minutes if the machine failed or the batteries ran out or the controller stopped working. He could die if the wound became infected and the infection travelled up to his heart. The enormity of it all was overwhelming.

Gemma was enthusiastic about the device, encouraging and supportive.

"Many of our LVAD patients are able to lead really normal lives. They return to work, ride bikes, go walking, and even have children," she said, "and remember it's not forever. It's a bridge to transplant, until you're well enough."

"You can't swim, or shower," said Andrew sadly. "I love swimming."

"You *will* get used to it," she said.

But I wondered how we would ever get used to it. How Andrew would get used to a wire from his stomach so he couldn't sleep on his left side, remembering to plug himself in, standing in the bathroom with wet wipes to clean himself, constantly worrying about people knocking into him or dropping the heavy bag hung from his shoulder and smashing the machine that kept him alive.

The following day, the LVAD specialist nursing team, Gemma and Mike, came to shorten the wire which ran from his stomach to the control device. The hospital kept the line longer until a patient was ready to leave as it needed to stretch to the monitors. Gemma said something to the nurses on the ward and they nodded and then she and Mike stood over Andrew inspecting the machine.

"On three," said Mike. "One, two, three," and then he pulled the main power lead from the device. An alarm blasted through the room, a deafening screeching sound. I looked to Andrew. The colour instantly drained from his face and he fell back onto the pillows.

"Andrew, are you OK?" I shouted. My heart was racing, and my hands began to shake. I saw panic spread across his face and utter fear in his eyes before they began to glaze.

"Yeah," he said softly, but I saw the life leaving him. I felt like I was watching him die. Those few moments felt like an eternity as his heart stopped working.

Gemma swiftly passed Mike a shorter wire. He grabbed it and fumbled for less than a second to connect it back into the mains.

"All done," said Mike, and the colour began to return to Andrew as quickly as it had gone. It could only have been twenty seconds, but it felt like forever. If we had needed confirmation of the importance of the LVAD, we had it now. In twenty seconds of it being unplugged Andrew had begun to lose consciousness, speech, and strength.

"You did well," said Mike. "Some people just black out straight away. You still have some residual heart function left. You would probably have enough time to change to controller or battery if something went wrong, and these are 99.9 per cent effective, but it's reassuring all the same."

I can't say I was reassured.

When they left, we looked at each other. I began to cry. "I'm sorry, I just feel emotional. It really scared me, and I never want to see that again."

"It scared me too," he said. "I never want to go through that either. The way I felt without the LVAD support was horrific. This machine is my lifeline. You really don't realise how important it is until it doesn't work."

Once the training was completed and the drains removed, Andrew was allowed to leave the ward for a few hours. The first time we walked across to the cafe, Darren and Lorraine were sat around a circular table with Lana and the lads. It felt strange that Andrew didn't know them. They shook his hand excitedly,

"It's so good to see you out of there, to see you doing so well," smiled Lorraine.

"We've heard so much about you. We feel like we know you," said Darren. "Well done on doing so well."

"We're going home on Monday," I said, "but please keep in touch. I want to know when Josh gets his new lungs and when he goes home too."

They smiled. "Of course," said Lana.

I took Andrew for a drive around the country lanes. Another night we went to the pub and out for dinner, each time returning him to the ward at the end of the evening to sleep, like he was living in a hotel.

Chapter Forty

On Monday 15th April, Andrew was discharged. It was different from before; he walked confidently along the corridor, carrying his LVAD in a shoulder bag, and out of the hospital door. He didn't pause to catch his breath or rest against the wall.

"I feel better than I have ever done since this started," he said. "I just didn't have the strength to do anything before. I was kidding myself. It was genuinely too much effort to lift a glass of water, to swallow, to move, but I had to convince myself. I understand now. I was really, really sick, and all the time you were only trying to help."

The first night he slept beside me, I woke panicked every hour, fearing I had heard the alarm sound and checking he was breathing. I knew it would take time before I finally relaxed.

We adjusted tentatively to the LVAD. I sometimes forgot the bag with the spare battery and controller and we argued over whose responsibility it was. But on the whole we were positive. We talked about us both returning to work and having a normal life again. He started looking at houses for sale and made enquiries at the gym. We attended the hospital every few days for check-ups, and as Andrew spoke to the doctors or underwent scans, I went to find Lana to ask about Josh.

"Still the same," she said sadly, "but I don't know how much more time we have."

"It will be OK," I said, the tears welling in my eyes. "There were so many times I thought Andrew wouldn't make it, but he did and Josh will too."

Andrew and I waited in the clinic for hours on end until at the end of the day we were reassured that his condition was moving in the right direction.

"My aim is to get as strong and physically fit as I can possibly be in this next six months to a year, so that when we get the call for the heart transplant, I'm in the best condition," he said.

"You know it could take longer," I said.

"I know, but it could take less time," he said, "and as long as I'm fit and healthy, the operation won't be as bad this time."

He took this seriously and every day I saw improvements. To me he looked a million times better than he had, but to everyone else he still looked severely unwell. He was underweight and pale. He had scars in his neck and scars on his arms. In truth, he looked like a drug addict, and it was shocking how some strangers treated him.

In the bank the cashier looked at him with disdain when he asked about taking out a large loan to buy a new car. "I'm not sure that's appropriate," she said dismissively, without checking the system.

"Check my record," he said, "and you will see I am a valuable customer."

She rolled her eyes and tapped a few digits into the screen.

"I've been very unwell," he said, "but I am on the mend now."

As his details flashed on the screen, her entire demeanour changed. "Of course, Mr Britton. I'm sorry. I-I-I must have been having a bad day. Would you like to become a premier customer?" she asked hopefully, backtracking.

On another occasion we went to the supermarket in the pouring rain. We couldn't park close to the entrance and we walked across the car park, soaking wet. Once inside the supermarket, Andrew suggested we sit down. He pulled up a chair close to the door.

"Shall I just nip round and grab the few things we need and then we can go?"

"That's a good idea," he said.

I quickly negotiated the store, one eye on Andrew, hastily throwing things into the basket, not paying attention.

When I returned to where he was sat, he was pale and green.

"I don't feel well at all," he said.

I tipped the contents of a carrier bag on to the floor and handed it to him just in time. He vomited violently, while the other shoppers walking past looked on unsympathetically, averting their eyes.

"I need to go home, but I can't walk to the car," he said.

"Are you OK if I leave you for just a few minutes? I'll get the car."

I ran across the car park in the pouring rain, jumped into the car and drove quickly outside the shop. I left the car running outside the front and hurriedly, carefully, helped him outside and into the passenger seat, soaked to the skin.

I started crying as we pulled away.

"Why are you crying?"

"It's just all so much. I just feel so stressed. I'm not sure I can do this. I'm so worried all the time. Something simple like going to the supermarket has become incredibly stressful."

"How do you think I feel?" he asked softly. "I can't do anything I did before. I have a wire coming out of my stomach. I can't bath. I can't wash. People look at me like shit. How do you think I felt seeing everyone watching me in disgust? This is not me. This is not my life. I was well respected in my job, and now everyone only speaks to me with sympathy and concern or thinks I'm some fucking druggie with the scars in my neck. I loved cycling and running and squash. Exercise was who I was, but I can't ride a bike with this round my neck. How can I run with this bag and equipment? How can I play squash? I want things to be normal. I want to be me again, but it's so fucking hard. Sometimes I think about just going in to a field and ending it all."

I stopped the car and held him tightly. "Never ever talk about ending it all. Don't you dare! Not after how much we've been through and how hard I fought to save your life. I love you. I'm so proud of how strong and how brave and positive you've been. No one should ever go through this, and you've done it and you've got through it and you're alive and we've been given a second chance. We will get through this and we'll find other things that will make you happy. It doesn't have to be sport. We'll find something else. I love you, Andrew. I love you. Don't you dare leave me!" I wiped my eyes with my sleeve and buried my head into his bony chest.

"I won't," he whispered into my hair.

Chapter Forty-One

On the second week, Andrew went for a drive with his friend Darren.

"He's got a new car," he said. "I'll be a few hours."

I suspected nothing. Jenny and Fraser had returned home and we had settled into a relatively stable rhythm of hospital appointments, dressing changes, eating and exercise. We had seen on the news about a new trial starting at Harefield at the end of the year for LVAD patients, which used stem cells to significantly improve heart function to the point where the LVAD could be removed and the patient would not need a heart transplant. We were advised that Andrew would be able to take part in this. It was a light at the end of the tunnel and a point to aim for.

"You need to be realistic," said Jane, "it might not happen."

"We have to have hope." I said. "It's the only thing that has kept me going for the last six months. Without hope, we have nothing."

I was less stressed and more positive than I had been in months and Andrew was the same. We were strangely happy considering the situation. Andrew was tired and grey and his stomach was distended, but we put it down to the medication needing to settle. He wasn't half as ill as he had been before. He could walk up the stairs and walk from the car park to the hospital. He could speak without pausing to take laboured breaths and his eyes were brighter. The doctors did not seem too concerned, and the LVAD was 99.9 per cent effective after all.

That evening, I watched him return and walk slowly to the door. He was carrying something in his arms. I stared more closely. He was holding a puppy. My very first thought was, "Darren's got a new dog." I opened the door to Andrew and he passed the puppy into my arms. It was a tiny tan-coloured English bull terrier with white socks and tummy and a long white nose. Her ears were huge and floppy and her eyes were bright and alert.

"You said I needed to find something to make me happy," he said. "This is Billy. She's ours. We've always wanted an English bull terrier and here she is."

"Have you gone mad? Are you having me on?"

"No. She's our puppy. She's a little friend for me while I'm recovering. She'll keep me company and make sure I exercise. It's perfect."

"This is not a good time, Andrew. You've only been out of hospital two weeks."

"It would never be a good time for you. You're so negative, and we've always wanted one of these, and you said I needed to find something to make me happy."

"But not now, not at this point. We've only just found our feet. Have you got food? Bedding? Toys? A collar? We'll need vets, insurance, a lead, bowls, dog guards. It's such a lot of responsibility. Have you even thought things through? Why didn't you at least discuss this with me? I can't tell you how cross I am."

"Not yet. She'll be OK tonight," he said, passing me a tin of puppy food from the garage, a soft toy and a blanket with paw prints on.

"This is ludicrous."

"I'm tired," he said. "I've only just had an operation. I don't need you going on at me. I'm going to lie down."

I looked at the tiny puppy in my arms. She gently licked my hand and her tail began to wag. I put her outside to go to the toilet and I opened the can of puppy food and poured it into a dish. I found a plastic bowl and filled it with water.

"I have no idea what I'm doing," I said to her. "Your daddy is an idiot, and I'm sorry but you won't be staying."

I called my friend Kate for advice. "Don't put her outside until she's had her jabs," she cried. "Has she had her jabs? Do you even know?"

I rushed outside and picked her up.

"And don't feed her any old puppy food. You need to know what she has been fed by the breeder. If you change her food, it can make her very sick."

I tipped the food into the bin.

"And I don't have a bed."

"Get a large drawer, empty it out, line it with newspaper and towels and put it in the kitchen; she'll feel safe in there."

I bought the right food from the vet and checked her immunisations. I spent the first night on the floor in the kitchen lying by the puppy's bed, stroking her to sleep as she whimpered. She climbed out of the bed and snuggled into my arms, nuzzling my neck and gently licking my face, and I cursed Andrew because I knew I couldn't let her go.

"That's Josh's favourite dog," said Lorraine a few days later. We had met her and Lana in the hospital reception.

"How is he?" I asked.

She looked down and shook her head a little. "He's not so good," she said quietly. "We're still waiting for a donor, and as every day goes on, he's losing more strength."

"I'm so sorry. I hope you get a match really soon," said Andrew.

"So do we," said Lana, the tears welling in her eyes, "but it's so good to see you so well."

"Josh will be the same," I said. "Please let me know when he has the operation. We can't stop thinking about you."

It was only hours later that I received a text from Lana. "Josh has a match! He's going into surgery now. I know he can do it!" followed by, "The operation went well. He's OK."

I anxiously checked my phone every hour to hear of Josh's progress.

On the third day, I received a text from Lana first thing in the morning before we got up.

"Josh has passed. He fought so hard. The lungs just didn't come in time. We're devastated."

I swallowed hard and re-read the message. He had been through so much in his short life and he shouldn't have gone. He shouldn't have been taken from them. I began to sob, my face pressed into the pillows.

"What's happened?" asked Andrew.

"Josh, he's died."

He held me tightly and stroked my head. I felt his shoulders shake as he began to cry.

"It's not fair," he whispered. "He was so brave. The family must be destroyed. It's heartbreaking and there was nothing anybody could do."

We held each other a little tighter that night, and I remembered Josh smiling as Peggy Sue waved at him through the window. They were such a kind and loving family, ripped apart cruelly. Their lives would never be the same again. There would always be a space where Josh should have been.

"That could have been me," said Andrew. "Why Josh and not me?"

"I don't know," I whispered.

His death hit us hard. It made us realise how important organ donation was. I had heard three people a day died waiting for a transplant, but to see it first-hand was shocking. It was suddenly more than just a statistic. I tried to think of things I could do to raise the profile and encourage more people to join the register. I saw an advert for a short film-making competition on the wall in the clinic. The film needed to promote the importance of letting your loved ones know you had signed up as an organ donor, as even if you have registered, your family have the final say. I had never made a film in my life, but I started thinking of ways I could pass the message on. I wrote a light-hearted script about a sock puppet called "Odd Socks and Organ Donation", and my friends Matt and Jez helped me to film it in the kitchen. I submitted it online and crossed my fingers.

Chapter Forty-Two

My friend Kate's birthday was on 9th May. Andrew's mum had come to stay so that I could go out to dinner with Kate and her family. Jenny and Andrew went to the hospital to attend the clinic, while I got ready, but they returned only half an hour later.

"They say I've got an infection, and they want to keep me in," Andrew said. "I've got to pack a bag for a few days until they can find the source and get rid of it."

We returned to the hospital and he was admitted onto Fir Tree Ward. He brought only a handful of items as he believed he was only staying a day or so and settled into a similar room to the one he'd had before only one floor above.

I had a bad feeling right from the start. Bloating had always been a clear sign of heart failure. I spoke to a nurse in the corridor. "Please be honest with me. Do you think it's something more serious than an infection but you don't want to scare us yet?"

She shook her head. "It's really common to get infections when you first have the LVAD operation. Honestly, don't worry. The LVAD is highly effective, 99.9 per cent effective."

I returned to the room, reassured. The next few days passed as they had done before. The doctors tried to establish what was wrong. They undertook test after test. Jenny and I sat beside his bed and watched the television fixed high on the wall.

"I am worried that you have heart failure again," said the doctor, finally, after the test results had returned. The familiar feeling of fear and tension filled my throat. "We are worried that the right side of your heart is not working properly, but we'll need to do a procedure to look into this more."

"What does this mean then?" asked Andrew.

"You will need a heart transplant more urgently than expected."

"But what about the trial?" I asked.

The doctor shook his head.

The next few days passed in a blur of confusion. We were told categorically that Andrew did not fit the criteria to be put onto the urgent heart transplant list. We were then subsequently told Andrew would be put on the list, and then by another doctor that he definitely would not be put on the list as there were too many patients on the list already. We didn't know whether to be relieved or anxious from one hour to the next. Was it a good thing that he wasn't sick enough to go on the list, or was it better for him to go on the urgent list as he would ultimately need a transplant? His regular doctor was incredibly understanding and supportive, keeping us updated of every change, but it was exhausting.

He was put on infusions to reduce the water in his stomach and the pressure on his heart. He was attached to milrinone again to improve his heart function but this time into his arm and not into his neck. I knew at this point that he would have to go onto the urgent heart transplant list. I remembered Warren's words. "You cannot take milrinone orally." I knew Andrew would not leave the hospital until he got a transplant. I could not think of the alternative.

Eventually, on May 23rd, the doctors said that Andrew would be placed on the urgent heart transplant list. The senior surgeon came to speak with us and talked us through his plan. He hoped that a match would be found in time. If not, the alternative was a machine that would support the right side of his heart. There were two machines. One lasted for around seven weeks and he would be bedbound in the intensive care unit, and then, if still no match had been found, they could fit a VAD (ventricular assist device) to the right side of his heart. The VAD would mean that Andrew would be able to return home with two battery packs either side of his waist. He would come off the urgent list and it could be years before he would be transplanted. Andrew looked at me in horror. We prayed that it would not come to this.

The transplant coordinator came to speak with us again. We

talked over the same things we had talked of before. This time it was easier to digest. It felt like déjà vu. We were advised that it would be a long wait due to the number of patients on the urgent transplant list.

"I won't be here long," Andrew said. But the days and weeks and then months passed quickly outside of his room.

I returned to work to try and make ends meet and give myself another focus other than the hospital, but I ran myself ragged trying to cope. My friends and family helped where and as often as they could, and my colleagues were kind and supportive. Jenny and Fraser came down for a few days every few weeks, but I was exhausted and emotional. I was awake at six in the morning to walk the dog, in order to get to work early to make up my hours. I paid a dog-sitter to look after her during the day and rushed back to walk her again after work. I tried to keep the house clean, tried to cut the grass, tried to complete all Andrew's washing and prepare his food and leave myself enough hours to spend quality time with him, staying at the hospital until 10pm.

He was kept inside for fear of infection, and we watched summer arrive and light up the skies. We saw the pink blossom on the trees fall across the pathways of the hospital and the grass grow taller and work on a new conservatory begin. The milrinone and diuretics improved Andrew's health significantly, but superficially, and we walked up and down the corridors in the evenings after work. He carried the LVAD and pulled the stand of infusions awkwardly alongside him, the wheels catching stiffly like a faulty supermarket trolley.

"I see you eyeing up my drip stand," said Robert, his neighbour in the corridor, who was also waiting for a heart transplant, smoothly pushing his infusions past. "I'll be sleeping with one eye open."

We laughed.

We paused at every window to watch the world outside. We saw the ambulances speed in and the staff rush to greet them, stretchers pulled from the back and patients like Andrew pushed quickly inside. We saw families smiling and families distraught. We recognised staff members and waved to our favourites as they crossed from the cafe. We read and re-read the cards on the noticeboards and patient booklets until we knew them off by heart. We paused at the single stone step at the end of the hall and stepped up and down: Andrew's exercise routine.

We chatted to the nursing staff. They were incredibly friendly and supportive, and we stopped at the rooms of the other long-term patients also waiting for heart transplants. They had been admitted around the same time as Andrew. Each story began differently; each ended the same.

Simon was a set builder for the film industry. He was in his early fifties with two children in their twenties and a lovely wife, Kim. Kim and I stood outside the hospital almost every evening, before walking inside, appreciating the freedom our other halves didn't have. We understood each other: the waiting, the worry, the panic, the fear.

"It won't be long now. Simon's got a theory. He thinks it's this week," said Kim. But months had passed and nothing happened.

Simon was always smiling. He was calm and relaxed. His heart problems had come on gradually; he began to feel breathless and tired. No one expected it. The family never thought of transplants until his heart function was too low to sustain his life. He spoke passionately about the work he did, desperate to get back. There were jobs booked for October and work he had to do. Daniel Radcliffe came to see him. I passed him in the corridor and recognised his face. Was he a relative or a canteen worker or a volunteer? It was only when Andrew excitedly told me that it clicked into place.

Robert was in his fifties and had long grey hair. He had a dry sense of humour and made hilarious deadpan comments to us and the nursing staff as he sat beside his bed and read. He told me that when he was first admitted, the TV was stuck on ITV4 for three weeks. He couldn't get anything but crime dramas and dated episodes of *Poirot*, and when they finally came to fix it, he was addicted, and the only channel he couldn't get was ITV4. So he read his books instead and tried not to think about the episodes he'd miss. He was a gardener. He had a dog, Chipper, whom he missed desperately, and a girlfriend, Sue, who came to see him on a Sunday. They completed the crossword together, as they would have done at the kitchen table. He'd had a heart attack at work. "The worst pain I've ever felt," he said. He was rushed to Harefield, but his heart was severely damaged and so he waited for a transplant too.

There was Geoff, who had been recently transplanted and was waiting to go home, a constant support to us all, and Phil whom I rarely saw. The other rooms were only occupied temporarily, and their residents came and went, but still Andrew and the others stayed week after week.

Andrew's days were filled by a constant stream of staff, visitors, cleaners and catering staff. The nurses took his blood first thing in the morning at 8am; his breakfast arrived and the cleaners came. His blood pressure and temperature were taken every two hours all day and all night, they changed the milrinone in his arm every three hours, and the furosemide every six hours. He had heparin in his wrist and he wore itchy heart rate monitors that never stuck properly to his chest and dropped off when he moved and the monitors alarmed.

Brian the volunteer came to see him at 10am. He had lunch at midday and doctor's visits and more checks in the afternoon. I arrived around 6pm and brought him his dinner, and we sat and watched TV and walked the halls until 9pm. Every evening when I left him, he stood illuminated in the large front window and waved sadly as I walked away, and every evening I tried not to cry as I walked to the car park.

At the weekends, the corridors were deserted and we became braver, climbing the staircases and exploring the hidden halls. We found the empty library and shut white doors with portholes and uneven wooden floors. We found the entrances to the balconies, glass-panelled doors padlocked shut. My friend at work had told me she had been at Harefield forty years ago, and in those days you were pushed in your bed out onto the balcony to breathe in the air.

"If only," said Andrew.

He leant out of the white wooden-framed windows that opened slightly and let a small breeze across his face. "If only I was allowed outside, I'd feel so much more human." But he never complained.

We spoke to the doctors and they agreed that infection no longer posed a risk to him, but they still wouldn't let him outside without a medical escort. The nurses were busy. They couldn't spare the time to take Andrew outside regularly. To their credit they tried as often as they could, sometimes missing breaks to allow Andrew fifteen minutes in the sun, but he felt guilty asking them when he knew they were short-staffed.

In the beginning, Robert, Simon and Geoff came outside too. We sat on the benches by the pavilion, and I brought the dog. They ate ice creams and chatted easily. Billy sat by Andrew's feet and chewed on thick white chewies held tightly between her paws. They were almost like workmates on a well-earned break; bound together, the four of them forged genuine friendships.

"I don't care who gets it first," said Robert. "I just want one of us to get a transplant soon."

Chapter Forty-Three

On a weekend circuit along the corridor, up the stairs, across by the balcony back down the stairs, I noticed another door.

"What if we go through here?" I asked Andrew.

Several stone steps led down to a fire door. A couple of nurses passed quickly through. I hid at the top of the stairs until I heard the door slam shut.

"It isn't alarmed either," I whispered. "It leads to the outside."

I sneaked down the stairs and opened the door; it led to a secret patch of grass around the side of the hospital, bright in the sunshine.

"But what about my heart rate monitor?" Andrew said. "Won't it alarm and panic the nurses if it goes out of range?"

"Let's see," I said. "Call it 'Operation ginger bull terrier'."

I loitered by the nurses' station, my eye on Andrew's heart monitor screen, making casual conversation as he tiptoed outside. His heart rate stayed steady. The signal wasn't lost.

"Mission successful," I whispered into my phone.

We stood on the steps and breathed in the outside.

"This feels amazing," said Andrew.

"Promise me you won't come outside on your own though. Make sure you always come with me, so if anything happens, God forbid, I can go and get help."

"Nothing will happen to me," said Andrew, smiling and winking.

I began to bring the dog to see Andrew regularly at the secret patch of grass. I saw more of the old Andrew; he had fight and determination, but he had softened too. I lay on the grass in the afternoons and he sat by my feet. We could have been any normal couple on a normal summer's day, except for the battery packs and controllers strapped to his side.

"It's still possible you'll be home for your birthday in August, if you get a match fairly soon."

He nodded. We never spoke directly about what the transplant meant. We spoke of a match in a detached way. It was too hard to face the truth of what it really meant. Someone needed to die for Andrew to live. We never discussed how much time he may or may not have left. I worried internally as the levels of medication increased. I remembered that Warren, his nurse in ITU, had mentioned that the body could only sustain the milrinone for a limited amount of time. I wondered how much more his body could take, but I stopped asking questions. It couldn't change anything. We just had to wait.

Sometimes we would hear the whirr of the helicopters above us and watch as the medical team landed on the helipad and rushed to ITU with precious cargo. It was hard not to feel overwhelmed with emotion. We wondered if Robert or Simon were about to receive their gift, but they were still sitting on their beds when we returned to the ward.

It was by the helipad that I first met Andrew's hospital room neighbour, Sue. She was reading a book about an English bull terrier as Billy and I were walking back to the car. I dropped her lead and she bounded towards Sue and jumped onto her lap.

"Billy!" I shouted apologetically, running to grab her collar.

"It's fine, I love dogs," said Sue. "I have two of my own. I miss them desperately when I'm in here."

Sue had had a double-lung transplant three years before. She was generally well, but her lung function had decreased. I started telling her our story and suddenly I couldn't stop. I'd held everything inside for so long and not spoken to anyone that I found myself tripping over my words to make sense of it all.

"It puts so much into perspective," she said. "It's all been so sudden. I knew my whole life that I would probably need a lung transplant, and it's a long time to prepare. You've had months. You need to let it out sometimes. You can't always keep this inside, only thinking about what's best for Andrew. Maybe make some contact with some groups? There are some really good ones on Facebook. Speak to other people who understand."

I nodded. A lot of the time I didn't feel like anyone could really understand. My friends were sympathetic and supportive, but it was so hard to explain what it was like to wake up every day with fear in my throat and the terrifying realisation that when I said goodbye to Andrew at the end of the day, it might be the last time I saw him.

Sue became a good friend. I valued her opinion. I joined an online group called Heart Transplant Families, and finally I was able to speak and engage with other wives and mothers and fathers and people who'd had heart transplants who understood me. It was amazing to hear the inspirational, incredible stories of families who had been through so much and still had the energy to help and support others, but it was hard when loved ones were lost. I cried for strangers' children and was overwhelmed by their strength. The group became friends, and I felt like they were waiting with us, willing us through. I met some of them sometimes in the canteen and I felt as though I'd known them forever.

Andrew's birthday came and went. Geoff went home, and Robert stopped leaving his room. Simon's condition became too serious to leave the ward. A darkness and discontent engulfed the men waiting on the ward. It was nearly five months. They were exhausted, confined, in pain and starting not to see an end.

"I would describe this as benign torture," said Robert. "I don't care who gets a transplant as long as one of us does soon. One of us needs to for the morale of us all, but at the moment I feel like we never will."

He never said, "I don't want to die in here," but I felt it as strongly as if he had said the words.

"I see the lights in Andrew's room go on in the middle of the night," he said. "He doesn't sleep either, none of us do."

And then one afternoon, Andrew called while I was at work.

"Simon's got a match!" he said. "I am so pleased for him, we all are!"

When I came to see Andrew in the evening, Simon was still in his room,

"When are you going down to surgery?" I asked.

He shook his head. "I'm not. Once they had done the checks, it wasn't quite right."

This happened again for Simon, the following night; again the heart wasn't right.

"They said before that they would never transplant a heart that wasn't 100 per cent, but it is disappointing," he said calmly.

"We need something good to happen," said Andrew.

We focused on fundraising and raising awareness about organ donation to detract from it all. Andrew's brother, Rob, swam pier to pier in Bournemouth in Speedos and waxed off body hair for every £1,000 he raised for the British Heart Foundation. His total reached £10,000 and everything came off. His friends and his mum and I cheered him on from the sandy beach. The sun shone brightly and the sea sparkled blue. For a few seconds I forgot everything and tried to pick out his bald head from the throng of swimmers.

Sometime later, I received a call telling me that the film I had made to raise awareness about organ donation had won the People's Choice Award. It had received the most views on YouTube, thanks to the tireless campaigning of my friends. I was invited to appear on the *Lorraine* daytime programme to promote the importance of organ donation for National Transplant Week.

The ward buzzed with excitement. The nurses asked me to give them a wave, and Andrew, Robert and Simon arranged to watch it together.

"Do us proud," said Robert.

The whole experience was entirely surreal. It passed in a flash. A car was sent to pick me up, and a lady from the NHS Blood and Transplant organisation met me in the reception area of the ITV studios. I was ushered to the make-up room, where a lovely lady spray-painted my face in foundation and brushed my hair. I sat in the green room as celebrities milled in and out, and I chatted with *Emmerdale*'s Wil Johnson, who was part of a large campaign to raise awareness about organ donation. When it was finally time to go on, Wil and I were greeted enthusiastically by Lorraine, who was warm and friendly. She held my hand tightly and smiled genuinely.

"How awful it's been for you both," she said. "Is he watching in hospital?"

I nodded and tried to keep it together.

"You just want your man home," she said.

Images of our wedding flashed on the screen and Wil and I answered questions about the importance of signing up to the organ donation register. It was an incredible opportunity, and I was so grateful to have had the chance to spread such an important message.

"You could have shed a tear," said Robert, smiling, when I returned to the hospital. "I was willing you to cry! It would have had more of an emotional impact!"

"You were amazing," said Andrew, tears welling in his eyes. "Let's hope this appeal means more lives will be saved and people like Josh will get a second chance."

Chapter Forty-Four

I had made a promise at the shrine in Bangkok that I would give blood if Andrew came home safely. I believed if I could save someone else's life, then somewhere, another family could save Andrew's in their most tragic time.

I am ashamed to admit I had never given blood before. I had gone to the blood-giving centres several times and pulled out at the last minute, scared of the pain and intimidated by the needles and the tubes filling with blood.

Andrew gave pints of blood every day. I watched as the nurses and doctors searched his arms for veins they were still able to use. Most were fibrous, thick and hardened and difficult to gain blood from. Desperately, they fed needles into his hand, his groin, and his feet; "Sharp scratch," they said, and he never complained. If he could do it every day, I could do it once.

The blood donation lorry was parked in the station car park. It was a bright summer morning. Jane and Emily accompanied me and there were people queued outside. Inside was a small waiting area with biscuits and squash. There were two beds either side, with people laying along them, flexing their hands and twisting their feet, their blood steadily streaming into the bags.

Andrew had spoken to a journalist a few days before. He called me as I sat waiting, filling in the blood donation forms.

"We're in all the papers!" he said excitedly. "Almost every single one! All the tabloids and the broadsheets. Can you get me some copies? We're even in the *Metro*."

Emily dashed to the front of the station and picked up a copy. We scrabbled through the pages to find the piece, and there he was on page five, a full-page spread. "I died six times on our honeymoon" read the headline above a picture of Andrew with the scar from the LVAD operation dark and thick from his collar to his waist. His pale skinny body was grey and drawn, every bone in his face protruding, his eyes wide and wired. It was the picture I had taken months ago just after the operation. I thought he had looked so well. He was smiling broadly. I remembered how grateful we were that he was alive.

I burst into tears and I couldn't stop crying. A lady opposite me reached over and patted my knee. "Is it your first time giving blood?" she asked kindly. "I was very nervous the first time too, but don't cry, it doesn't hurt at all."

I lay on the bed on one side of the lorry and Emily on the other. I stretched out my arm and the nurse carefully inserted the needle. It didn't hurt. I looked out of the window at the bright clear sky and the leaves on the trees gently waving in the wind, and I felt clearly that it was time for Andrew to get the transplant.

Afterwards, Emily and I and her small son went to a Buddhist monastery in the countryside near to where we lived. We lit incense as I had done in Bangkok and offered flowers from her mum's garden. I left a small ceramic elephant that I loved.

"I've fulfilled my promise," I whispered. "Please let Andrew Britton have a second chance. Let the transplant come tonight."

"Don't be disappointed if it doesn't happen," said Emily, as we drove back through the lanes.

"But it will," I said, certainly. "I know that it will."

When I went to bed, I wore the nightdress I had worn on our wedding night. I laid comfortable clothes on the chair, clothes I would wear while I was with him before he went down to surgery. Steve, our landlord, was staying. It felt like fate.

"Are you OK to take me to the hospital if it is tonight?" I asked.

"Of course," he said.

When the phone rang at 2am, I wasn't surprised.

"It's OK," Andrew said calmly, pausing for a moment. "They have found a match. They have already done the first few checks and it looks good. It looks like it's going to happen. Don't panic.

Don't rush. Sort the dog out, and then if you can come here, I want you to be here. I'll call my brother and my parents. I've spoken to Nick. Oh, and the surgeon on tonight is the surgeon who did my LVAD."

I thought I'd be terrified, but instead I felt calm and collected, even a little bit excited. This is what we had been waiting for, and finally the moment was upon us. Thoughts of the family who had lost someone flooded through my mind, but I had to stay strong.

I knocked on Steve's door. "It's time," I said, really ominously.

"Right. Shit. Ok. Right." He leapt from the bed. "I'll quickly put some clothes on and we'll head up there now."

I rang my friends Jeni and Amanda. "We're on our way," said Jeni. "We'll wait in the relatives' room until he goes down, and then we'll stay with you until he's had the operation and all is OK."

I must have arrived at the hospital at half two. I walked down the darkened corridors, lightly lit. I passed Robert's room and the door was open.

"What are you doing here?" he whispered.

"They've got a match."

"Thank God. You both deserve this," he said, hugging me. "I am so happy it's Andrew."

The nurses on the ward were visibly excited, smiling broadly, bustling about the ward station, completing forms, whispering quickly, answering the phone and nodding.

"It all looks good."

Andrew was sat in bed. He was composed. I hugged him tightly. I would not let myself think it could be the last time I would ever see him.

"We need to wait on two more tests," he said steadily, "and then I need to prepare for surgery, shave my chest, wash thoroughly, put my gown on, seal my wristbands and take the first dose of immunity suppressants that I'll take for the rest of my life."

Those last few hours we spent before the surgery were peaceful. I lay on the bed next to him and rested my head by his side. I listened to the whirr of the LVAD through his chest for the last time and stroked his face, trying to take in every last bit and commit it to memory. We watched the sun rise. We didn't speak much. We listened to our favourite songs, the first song at our wedding, our bed swimming songs. He unclipped the chain with his lucky penny and fed through his wedding ring (that still spun round his skinny finger) and secured it around my neck.

"They will keep you safe and bring you strength," he said.

I tried not to cry. Finally, the transplant coordinator came and said it was time to go. Andrew stood carefully and walked to the theatre bed to be transported to surgery.

I hugged him gently.

"It will be completely fine," he said.

"Do you want to go down with him?" asked the transplant coordinator as I stood by Andrew's bed.

"I want to do this on my own," said Andrew, squeezing my hand. "You stay here, clear my room, get your friends, get some rest, and I'll see you in a few days. I love you the most."

"I love you too," I whispered, as they pushed his bed down the corridor.

Jeni, Steve and Amanda came to the room. It was 5am. He would not return to this room. He would be in intensive care for several days and then on the high-dependency ward.

"You can wait here," said the coordinator, "or you can go home, whatever you prefer. The operation can take up to eight hours. I can call you when we are halfway there, so you know what to expect."

I made phone calls to his parents, Rob and Karen, his friends, Brian the volunteer. The girls and Steve bagged and boxed Andrew's things around me, and then we made the journey home. Fraser and Jenny set off. Rob and Karen were in the car.

Emily and Rach came to the house with breakfast. We sat in the garden. It was warm and bright, still early. I tried to eat but I couldn't swallow. I showered in a daze, and my friends cleaned the house. I anxiously checked my phone for any information. The time passed slowly, every second took an age.

"Why don't we take the dog for a walk?" suggested Rach, and so we drove to a nature reserve five minutes from our house.

The dog dashed in and out of the reeds and we threw her ball into the lake. It felt entirely surreal. Occasionally, for just a moment, I forgot why we were there and felt happy to be surrounded by my friends in the sunshine, and then the realisation hit me a second later and my breath caught in my throat.

Rob and Karen arrived and we walked through the wide fields. Rob was understandably distracted. He kept his head down. He held Karen's hand tightly and hardly spoke.

We stopped at the wooden cafe cabin and ate ice creams in the sun. It was one o'clock in the afternoon. He had gone down to the theatre at five o'clock in the morning. I was counting the hours on my fingers when my phone rang shrilly – private number, the hospital. I felt the same fear as I had in the Maldives. Nervously, I answered.

"Mrs Britton," said the transplant coordinator, "there's been a problem. I need you to come to the hospital as quickly as you can. The surgeon needs to speak with you."

Rob and Karen could immediately see from my face that something wasn't right. I sat down and took a deep breath. "You're scaring me. I'm scared," I mumbled, hardly able to speak. "What's happened? What's happening? Please tell me now."

"It's OK," she said calmly, "but please come to the hospital. We will talk to you there. Come to the relatives' room in the corridor by ITU."

The relatives' room was where they told patients' families that their loved ones had died. I feared she would not tell me this information over the phone. Terrible, dark, terrifying thoughts flooded my mind. I was shaking and panicked. I couldn't stand for a second, and then the adrenalin kicked in and I leapt to my feet. I needed to know, whatever the outcome.

My friends took the dog. They said they sat in silence in the car, no one daring to speak.

Rob, Karen and I stumbled to Karen's car. I sat in the front, clasping my hands, begging, praying, willing Andrew to be alive, to please let him be alright, please let him be OK. The journey took an age. Five minutes felt like fifty, as we queued at junctions and trailed behind learner drivers. Karen dropped Rob and me at the hospital entrance and we flew from the car, bursting through the doors and down the corridor, running as quickly as we could. I buzzed the Tannoy in the waiting room and we went through the relatives' room, my heart beating outside of my chest, tears streaming down my face. Rob held my hand tightly.

The surgeon walked calmly into the room. He sat down opposite us with the transplant coordinator.

"Lauren, why you crying?" he asked in an Italian accent. "Andrew, he is fine."

Rob and I looked at each other, and half laughed, half sobbed an exhalation of panic and stress and fear and relief.

"The heart, it was not good enough," he said. "Andrew, he is in ITU, sedated, intubated, catheterised. We were ready to start, and then the new heart, it began to worry me. We use a machine. It is called an Organ Care System. It allows us to watch the heart as if it was in a new body. Tubes profuse the heart with blood, they keep it pumping, and we can monitor how the heart works. At first it was fine – that was why we got so far – but then it began to display signs I did not like. Very tiny, minor signs, but it did not look right. I asked the opinion of the other surgeons. We watched the heart for five hours. We watched how it worked and we watched these signs and then finally we decided we would not go ahead with the operation. My job, it is all about risk. If Andrew was more unwell, I would have taken the risk. If the risk had been greater for him to wait for another heart I would have undertaken the surgery. But he is fit. He can wait."

I smiled weakly, desperately trying to take it all in, the adrenalin still surging through me, my head thumping.

"It's disappointing, but reassuring to know that you would not transplant unless it was perfect and he can wait," said Rob. As always, he understood. "Has this ever happened before?"

"Only once in fourteen years did we get to the surgical table," said the surgeon. "But on the other occasion we had already made the incision. He is lucky we did not make the cut. I know he will be angry and upset, but he must know that this was not his time. His time will come, and I want the heart for Andrew to be perfect."

"When will you wake him?" asked Robert.

"About an hour or so."

"I want to be there when he wakes up," I said.

I imagined him coming round: intubated in ITU, emotional, relieved he'd had the surgery and then to be told it had not gone ahead. I knew he hated the breathing tubes, the catheter and the wires in his neck. I knew how excited he was to not have the LVAD, to not be terrified of the batteries running out and the machine inside him failing. He would be devastated. It broke my heart to think of his initial happiness and then the disappointment when he realised.

I called my friends and we sat in the hospital grounds. Jenny and Fraser arrived and we drank tea in the sunshine and nobody spoke. No one knew what to say. We waited for the call to say they were waking him up, and when my phone finally rang, Jenny and Fraser looked at me.

"You go first," said Jenny. "He'll want to see you first."

Andrew was already awake. The staff had removed the breathing tubes and he was propped up on the bed with piles of pillows. He was pale and drowsy but able to speak croakily.

"You OK?" I asked.

He nodded.

"I knew when I woke up. I felt my neck first, to see if I had a tracheotomy. That was my biggest fear. I thought, no trachea, that's a good sign, and then I felt the weight of the LVAD beside me, and I properly panicked for a second and thought the surgery may have gone so wrong that they'd had to do a LVAD for the new heart. And then I felt my chest for the incision and my scar was the same. There was no gauze across the wound and I realised the operation hadn't gone ahead. The surgeon came to see me and he explained. It makes me feel better to know he is fighting for me. It's just," he paused and his eyes filled with tears, "what about the donor family. They thought their loved one's heart would be used. It would save someone else, and it hasn't been. I feel devastated for them at this terrible time. I don't care about myself. I feel like it would have given them comfort and now it won't."

He started to cry.

I held his hand tightly and stroked his head. "What they did was an amazing thing. It won't be forgotten."

"I just feel for them. I couldn't think about the donor or the family until now, and now it hits you squarely when it's suddenly real."

Three hours later, he returned to Rowan Ward, back to his old room. We brought back the bags of belongings, dragging them along the corridor. I paused at Robert's room. He was reading intently but eased to his feet as I stopped at his door.

"How is he doing?" he asked.

I shook my head. "Got to surgery, but then didn't go ahead."

Robert turned his head away. I saw his eyes fill with tears.

"It isn't fair," he said. "I feel worse than if it was me who had the disappointment. I'm an old man. I've lived my life, but Andrew, he's so young, he's got so much of his life left to lead. I really thought this was the beginning of the rest of your lives. I-I'm so sorry, Lauren. I'm absolutely devastated."

I shook my head. "His time will come, as will yours and Simon's. It wasn't the right time. It wasn't the right heart. It can't be long now."

He shook his head sadly.

"Give him my best," he said.

Chapter Forty-Five

It's hard to explain what it's like to spend seven months in hospital, day after day after day stretching out in front of you. I tried to understand but I don't think I could fully appreciate what it felt like to only see four walls and a corridor and occasionally the outside for weeks on end, and the weeks kept passing and the chance of Andrew ever leaving felt less and less.

The urgent heart transplant list kept growing. A young Irish girl, Louise, who was pretty and bright, and smiley and positive, joined the group of waiters and eased the mood a little, but it was hard for anyone to see a light at the end of the tunnel.

And then suddenly a few days after Louise had arrived, Robert got a call to say that they had found a suitable donor. He was in the corridor on the bed, ready to be moved to surgery, when I arrived in the afternoon. I hugged him. "I'll miss your miserable face."

"Andrew will be next," he said.

The operation went well. There were some complications but he was a fighter. Sue, his girlfriend, was called a few days after surgery when the surgeons feared they might have to operate again, but the medication was adjusted and his condition improved. Andrew and I were able to visit him a week or so later. He was thin and drawn and his hands shook as he spoke, but he shone with happiness and relief.

"I'd recommend this to anyone," he said. "I feel bloody amazing."

The next morning, I woke with a sense that something would happen. On my way to work, I heard our favourite songs on the radio. The ones we had listened to before the false alarm. It felt like a sign. I told my colleagues I had a feeling it would happen that day.

At five o'clock, I very nearly set my email out of office alert, but then feared it would tempt fate. I left my shopping in the fridge and cursed because I knew I would not be back to get it for weeks.

It was still light when I arrived at the hospital, and Andrew and I sat outside in our secret place. The sun was fading slowly and he reached for my hand.

"Louise, she got her transplant this morning," he said. "Of course, I'm happy for her, I'm really happy for her, but she's waited a few weeks and I've been here nearly ten months now. There just comes a point when you think, I can't keep waiting anymore. How many people do you think kill themselves waiting, how many people just unplug the LVAD, how many people just reach a point when they can't wait anymore?"

"None," I said. "No one. Please don't give up. Please don't talk like this. It will come, I promise. I feel like tonight's the night. I've laid out my hospital clothes like before, my wedding nightdress. I feel it's tonight."

He shook his head. "I hate it when you say it might be tonight. The longer I've waited has no bearing on how long I will continue to wait. It's complete and utter chance that some poor cyclist will come off their bike and their details will match mine. I'm not willing anything to happen to anyone, and if I get my hopes up, they'll only be dashed again. We wait. That's what we do, and it will be one day, but don't put timescales on it. What will be, will be."

We went back to his room and flicked through the television channels. It was nearly half past nine when we heard a knock at the door.

"Can I come in?" asked the transplant coordinator.

"Of course," we said in unison.

"We have a match," he said. "Initial investigations look good. They are sending out a team. We'll know more in a few hours, but the signs are good this time."

"Thank you, OK, thank you," said Andrew.

"Out of interest, who is the surgeon on duty tonight?" I asked.

"The surgeon who performed your LVAD operation," said the transplant coordinator, "but all of the surgeons are excellent."

"He is our favourite," I said.

Andrew and I looked at each other. "It feels right this time, doesn't it?" he said.

As before, we sat on the bed. He paced a little, then showered and shaved again. I still wore his penny and his ring around my neck. I hadn't taken them off. The surgical staff came to see Andrew and asked him to sign the paperwork, and then the anaesthetist arrived.

"This time they will not sedate you until they are 100 per cent certain that they will go ahead. It won't happen again like before," he said.

Andrew and I lay on our sides on his single hospital bed, pressed against each other. We listened to music and looked out at the night. He took the first dose of immunity suppressants just before the hospital porters came to take him to the theatre. I kissed him gently and held his hand until the last second, and then they wheeled him away. He was so incredibly brave. I felt hot tears stream down my cheeks.

"I'll be fine," he mouthed.

"I'll call you when we are halfway there," said Rachel, the LVAD nurse, "but I estimate it will be around eight hours before he's out."

Jeni and Amanda helped me clear his room. We returned home and the three of us tried to sleep, but I was wired. I was shaking. My heart felt unsteady. I struggled to breathe. I called Andrew's parents, Rob and Karen, my parents and Brian the volunteer again. This time I didn't want to be too far from the hospital. If something happened, I wanted to be there.

Rach and Emily arrived and I tried to eat but couldn't swallow.

"Just try," they pleaded, "it'll make you feel worse." But I shook my head and just concentrated on keeping as steady and as calm as I could. Breathe in, breathe out.

We sat in the hospital canteen. We sat in the waiting area. We sat on our secret grass and on the field by the horses and the helipad. Every minute seemed like an eternity, and I had eight hours to get through.

At ten o'clock in the morning, the nurse called me to say the LVAD had been removed successfully, but it had taken a long time as it was very "stuck down". He was on the bypass machine and they would start the procedure very soon.

"I'll call you again at lunchtime," she said.

My palms were clammy and my phone slipped from my hand, and I clutched it so tightly my knuckles coloured. "Would you say twelve is lunchtime?" I asked the girls.

"I'd say one," said Amanda, and so I waited until one.

"What about now?"

"Lunchtime could technically be up to two," said Jeni, and so we waited another hour on the field by the helipad.

By three o'clock I was beginning to panic. I feared things had gone wrong. Terrifying thoughts filled my head and I pushed them aside, but they kept coming back. I bit my fingers and twisted my hair and ground my teeth. I was shaking and tearful. I struggled to speak or breathe. I was verging on hysteria.

"Go to his old room and ask if they have any news," said Rach, and they held me upright and we walked to the ward.

The sister on duty took me into a side room.

"When they are in surgery we can't contact them," she said calmly. "Please try not to worry. Sometimes it takes a long time. As soon as I know anything, I will let you know."

We returned to the field and sat in the fading sun. Emily's baby had a small football and the five of us played catch and piggy in the middle to pass the time. We were a strange nervous group, close to tears, desperately trying to stay upbeat until we received any news.

Just before 5pm, Jeni, Amanda and Rach went to the cafe to get a coffee. My phone began to ring in my hand and "private number" flashed on the screen.

"Lauren, it's Rachel, the LVAD nurse. He's fine. He's in ITU in the bed by the nurses' station."

"Is he OK? Is he really OK?" I stumbled over my words, hardly able to speak or process the information.

"Yes he's fine. You can come and see him in half an hour, once he's settled in."

"He's OK!" I screamed at Emily. "He's had the operation! He's OK! He's OK!"

She hugged me tightly, tears streaming down our faces.

The others walked towards us, dropping their coffees in panic as they saw our tearful faces.

"He's OK, He's OK!" I shouted. "He made it! He's OK."

The next few minutes passed in a flurry of excited and emotional phone calls. Jenny and Fraser and Rob arrived at the hospital in minutes and hugged me tightly.

I can't remember what we said. I just kept repeating, "He's OK, He's OK," and Jenny and Fraser steadied themselves, relieved, emotional, overwhelmed and desperately aware of another family somewhere in the depths of unimaginable grief.

We had been given a second chance through the kindness of strangers, the gift of life. The enormity, the kindness, made us shake with sobs.

Half an hour later, we were able to visit Andrew in ITU. We walked along the glass corridor and the sun shone brightly through the windows. The staff bustled in and out and the alarms rang and the machines beeped, and Andrew was lying asleep on the bed by the nurses' station. He had wires in his neck and tubes in his throat and drains by his bed and a stack of infusions above his head, but he looked amazing and alive. His chest rose and fell and his colour was good. There was no LVAD by his side.

"He is doing very well," said the surgeon. "The chest, it was very difficult to open. It took me four hours to open the chest and remove the LVAD and just half an hour to put in the new heart. The operation, it was difficult, very complicated, but he is fine. We will monitor him very closely, but he is doing very well. If he continues like this, we will look to wake him tomorrow morning."

I slept fitfully and fearfully the first night, but my phone didn't ring, and Jenny, Fraser, Katie and I were able to visit him at eleven the following morning.

"You go first," said Jenny and Fraser.

"Together," I said, and so the three of us walked through to the ward.

His eyes were open as we approached his bed. He reached out his hand towards his parents and me.

"We did it," he whispered. "Thank you, my donor. Thank you, my donor's family."

He turned his head slightly and motioned for us to move forward, so we were close to his face.

"Never forget I love you, and I love you and I love you."

Epilogue

On 25th December 2012, at 02:00, I had my sixth heart attack. I was awake. I knew what was happening. The medical team surrounded my bed and a nurse stoked my head while the doctor explained that they needed to shock me. The pads got placed onto my chest. They stood back. Then they hit the button. It felt like a release. The air was forced into my chest and my body bounced on the bed and left my ears ringing. My heart had very nearly stopped again, but they got it just in time. Within an hour I had a cup of tea and rang my wife and muttered, "They had to shock me again."

That was the sixth heart attack I had.

As I write, it's only seven months since I was gifted life by a stranger's family. It's hard to express the gratitude that I and my family have for them and for all those involved in keeping me safe and putting me back together. It is truly humbling. When the story hit the national press, I got a lovely card. It simply said, "Strangers do care and we wish you the best." There were so many moments that I had no medical right to survive. I got friendly with my surgeon, who did all my operations, and after the transplant I saw him in passing and he said that I must have "someone looking over me." He was right. I spent a year in hospitals in three different countries, had six heart attacks, two balloon pumps, one ICD, one LVAD and finally a transplant. While it seems cruel to have everything taken so dramatically and quickly, I was lucky. Physically I was lucky. I was fit, strong, young, and my body could take the punishment. However, I was even luckier with the strength I got from family, friends and strangers. Everyone was looking over me.

I came to terms with my own death. I never thought I would die, but I accepted my situation. Being told you need an urgent transplant now seems shocking. At the time I thought how much more can be thrown my way? Little did I know there was so much more to come. But this story is not about me. It's about courage, support and kindness. It's also about how amazing the NHS is. We hear stories in the press about failing hospitals, but Harefield Hospital is full of people that show the best our country has to offer. I had an Italian surgeon, Spanish, Greek, British doctors, Indian, Polish, Nigerian, Thai, Czech nurses and support staff from all over the world. The NHS is a fantastic example of the best a multicultural open immigration society offers.

I learnt a lot about myself. I learnt that I was strong, but you have to reach out when you need help. I would be dead if it was not for my wife. No ifs, buts or maybes, just dead. She fought to keep me alive throughout the whole year and was an absolute rock. I love you.

My family never gave up hope and were there every step of the way. I was having a cup of tea with my mum in hospital and she said that she would do anything to swap places with me and would happily give up her own life for mine. She just didn't want to see me in any more pain. My dad would tell me every day that he loved me and that I was his hero. The feeling was always mutual. My brother Rob and his partner Karen kept us all sane at times when there seemed no hope. Again, I love you both.

Life now is different. I'm still adjusting. I have good days and then I have not-so-good days. Physically I'm getting stronger. Mentally, it's tough. But I'm glad I have these problems now. Lots of people ask if I'm OK now. I always say, "I'm getting used to my new normal."

If you're reading this and not sure if you have registered as an organ donor, please check. Registering is simple and quick and it does save lives. While I was waiting for my transplant, people on the same ward died. I was lucky. Others were not and ran out of time on "the wait". If there is one thing that I can do now, it is to ask people to register. Have a conversation with your family to say that if the worst ever happened, you want to help others to live. Potentially, one donor can save five people.

Every day I think of my donor and their family. It is the ultimate expression of kindness. Thank you.

Fate nearly took my life, but then gifted it back again. Perhaps it's fitting that fate has the last word. Just out of hospital, I was in our kitchen at home when I heard Lauren running down the stairs screaming, "I'm pregnant!" We hugged, and tears of pure joy ran down both our faces. We had been advised that it may be difficult for us to fall pregnant due to the drugs I take. It felt like a miracle. We are expecting our first little baby in October 2014. A stranger's life gave me back mine, and now Lauren and I have been able to make life.

Our Wedding Day

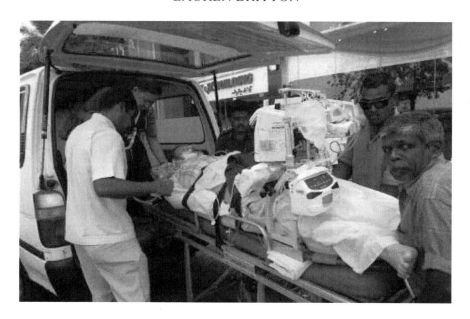

Transfer from the Male hospital to the airport.
Tholal is wearing a purple T-shirt.
I asked them to untuck Andrew's feet.

All the team loading Andrew onto the ferry.

The Thai team, loading Andrew onto the jet.

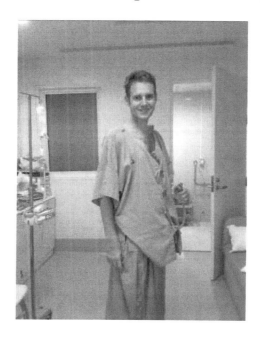

The picture I took in Bangkok when Andrew first stood up.

**Rob, Fraser, me and Jenny on Christmas Day,
just before we found out Andrew had had a heart attack.**

**Some of the nurses in Thailand with Andrew and me, making
the peace sign, just before we left for the UK.**

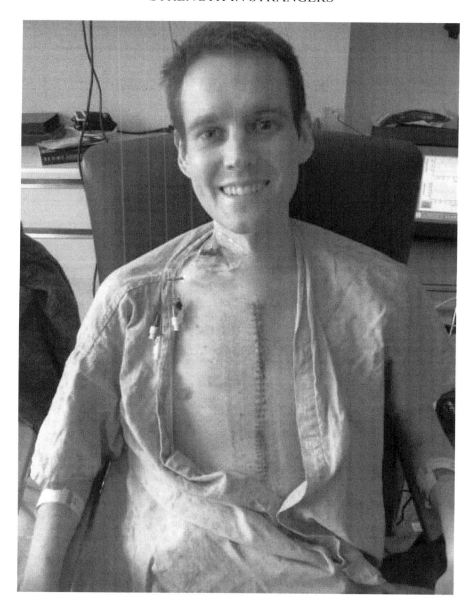

Andrew, after the LVAD operation.

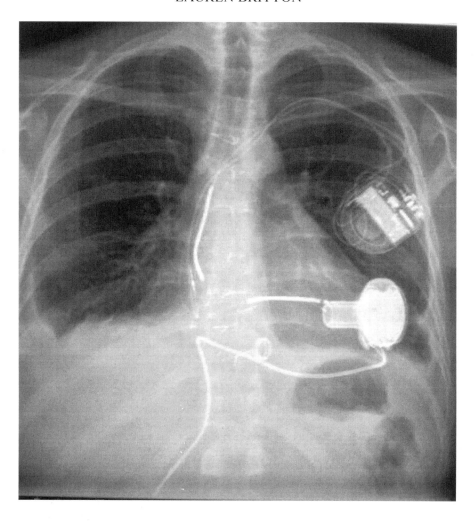

An X-ray of Andrew's chest, showing the LVAD and ICD.

Billy, the first day she arrived.

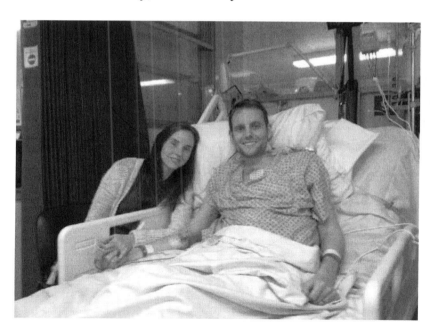

Andrew, after the heart transplant operation.

Waiting in the sunshine at our secret exit at Harefield.

Frank Fabio, born 13th October 2014

24900588R00138

Printed in Great Britain
by Amazon